WEATHER · ELECTRICITY ENVIRONMENTAL INVESTIGATIONS

WRITTEN BY SANDRA MARKLE
ILLUSTRATED BY BEV ARMSTRONG

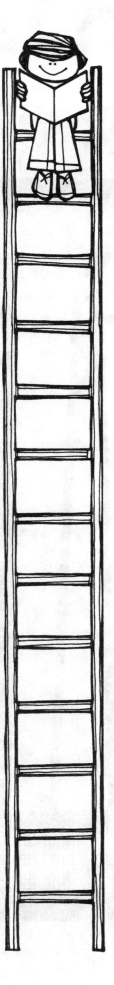

The Learning Works

CONTENTS

To the Teacher 5-6

Weather
Bulletin Board and Learning Center Ideas 7-8
Pretest 9
The Sun's Heat 10-11
What Makes the Wind Blow? 12
What Is the Coriolis Effect? 13
How to Make an Anemometer 14
How to Make a Wind Vane 15
Prevailing Winds 16-17
How to Make a Nephoscope 18
The Chilling Adventure 19
Land Puzzles 20
How to Make a Barometer 21
Water Vapor 22
Where Will Dew Form? 23
How Do You Make a Cloud? 24
Clouds Can Help Predict the Weather 25
How to Make a Hygrometer 26
How to Use Your Hygrometer 27
How to Make a Rain Gauge 28
What Does a Weather Map Tell You? 29-30
Making Your Own Weather Forecasts 31
Weather Records 32-33
Weather Brain Busters 34
Additional Information Sources and Correlated Activities 35-37
Posttest 38
Answers 39-40
Award 41

Electricity
Bulletin Board and Learning Center Ideas 42-43
Pretest 44
The Power of the Yellow Stone 45
What Is Electricity? 46
Which Charge Is It? 47-48
Can a Magnet Generate an Electric Current? 49-50
Power Challenge 51-52
Other Ways to Generate an Electric Current 53
What Is a Complete Circuit? 54
Conductors and Insulators 55
Circuit Puzzle 56
Series and Parallel Circuits 57
Circuit Testing 58
Battery Power 59-60
How Does a Switch Work? 61-62
You Can Make Your Own Light Bulb 63-64

Using Electricity to Copper Plate 65
Build Your Own Telegraph Set 66-68
The Morse Code Kidnapper 69
The Cost of Using Electricity 70
Can Taking a Shower Help Save Electricity? 71
Additional Information Sources and Correlated Activities 72-74
Posttest 75
Answers 76-77
Award 78

Environmental Investigations
Bulletin Board and Learning Center Ideas 79
Neighborhood Study Questionnaire 80
Pretest 81
What Is Happening to Our Environment? 82
Your Share of the Garbage 83
Take a Litter Look 84
Landfills 85-86
Do You Really Need It? 87
Incineraton 88
A Soapy Problem 89-91
Be Careful—It's Acid Rain 92-93
Help a Stream 94-95
Help a Stream Log 96
What's Happening to the Air? 97-98
Recycling 99
Follow the Glassphalt Road 100-101
Recycle Your Own Paper 102-103
Help an Environment 104
Additional Information Sources and Correlated Activities 105-107
Posttest 108
Answers 109-110
Award 111
Notes 112

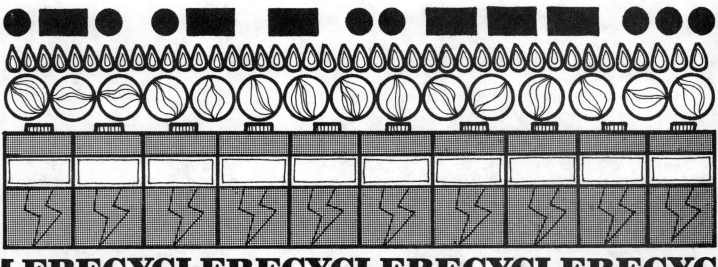

LERECYCLERECYCLERECYCLERECYC

TO THE TEACHER

The activities in this book have been selected especially for gifted students in grades 4 through 8 and are designed to challenge them and to help them develop and apply higher-level thinking skills. These activities have been grouped by subject matter into the following three sections: weather, electricity, and environmental investigations.

Weather

The weather section in this book includes activities to acquaint students with basic weather principles. Step-by-step instructions are given for making simple weather instruments, including an anemometer, a barometer, a hygrometer, a nephoscope, and a wind vane. Using these instruments, students can observe and measure present weather phenomena and predict future weather patterns with considerable accuracy. Also included are investigations in which students will learn how to read a weather map, how the sun affects the earth's weather, how landforms affect wind, how to determine prevailing winds, and how to use prevailing wind information in community planning.

Electricity

The activities in this section constitute a thought-stimulating exploration of electricity. They begin, just as early investigators did, with a study of static electricity. Students generate free flowing electrons to discover what electricity is and to find out about negative and positive charges. They become aware of a number of different ways in which an electric current can be created and have opportunities to build currents, test for conductors (or insulators), create and work circuit puzzles, and construct a two-way switch, a light bulb, and a telegraph set. Through these activities, students are also made aware of the tremendous demand our indiscriminate use of electricity makes on our available power resources and of the need to conserve.

Environmental Investigations

In this section, students will investigate the main ways in which people are damaging the environment. They will learn about landfills and incineration, about phosphates and acid rain, and about recycling and glassphalt. They will have opportunities to compare various trash and garbage disposal methods, to recognize things that are harmful to the environment, and to develop and implement practical solutions to man-made environmental problems.

Within each of these three sections are bulletin board ideas, learning center ideas, a pretest and a posttest, as many as twenty-seven activity pages, detailed directions for more than fifty activities, suggestions for additional correlated activities to extend learning, answer pages, and an award to be given to students who satisfactorily complete the unit of study. These materials may be used with your entire class, for small-group instruction, or by individuals working independently at their desks or in learning centers. Although you may want to elaborate on the information presented, each activity has been described so that students can do it without additional instruction.

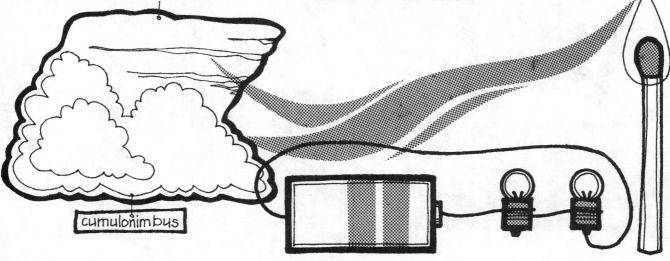

cumulonimbus

All of the activities in this book are designed to provide experiences and instruction that are qualitatively different and to promote development and use of higher-level thinking skills. For your convenience, they have been coded according to Bloom's taxonomy. The symbols used in this coding process are as follows:

● **knowledge** — recall of specific bits of information; the student absorbs, remembers, recognizes, and responds.

■ **comprehension** — understanding of communicated material without relating it to other material; the student explains, translates, demonstrates, and interprets.

▲ **application** — using methods, concepts, principles, and theories in new situations; the student solves novel problems, demonstrates use of knowledge, and constructs.

✳ **analysis** — breaking down a communication into its constituent elements; the student discusses, uncovers, lists, and dissects.

▬ **synthesis** — putting together constituent elements or parts to form a whole; the student discusses, generalizes, relates, compares, contrasts, and abstracts.

◉ **evaluation** — judging the value of materials and methods given purposes, applying standards and criteria; the student judges and disputes.

These symbols have been placed in the left-hand margin beside the corresponding activity description. Usually, you will find only one symbol; however, some activities involve more than one level of thinking or consist of several parts, each involving a different level. In these instances, several symbols have been used.

Electricity, weather, and the environment are separate but interrelated areas of human experience. Studied together, they will help students understand that the earth's resources are limited and precious. They will enable students to appreciate some of the discoveries and inventions of the past and encourage students to apply their ingenuity to dealing with the misuses and abuses of the present to prevent shortages in the future.

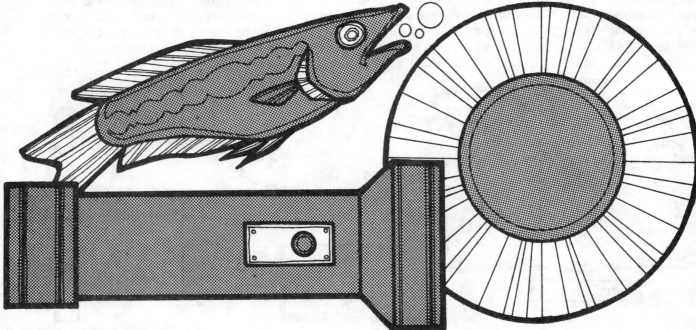

BULLETIN BOARD AND LEARNING CENTER IDEAS

1. Label a bulletin board **Weather Myths**. Cover the board with a collection of weather myths. Invite students to add family weather myths. During your study of this unit, discuss how some of these myths may have gotten started and what they mean.

> A circle around the moon;
> 'T will rain soon.
>
> When the cow scratches her ear,
> It means a shower is near;
> But when she thumps her ribs with her tail,
> Expect thunder, lightning, and hail.
>
> Red sky in the morning
> Sailors take warning.
> Red sky at night
> Sailors delight.
>
> The thicker the fur on woolly bear caterpillars,
> The worse the winter ahead.
>
> A lot of winter snow
> Means the summer crops will grow.
>
> Birds flocking together are a sign that a storm is coming.
>
> If the groundhog sees his shadow on Groundhog Day, there
> will be six more weeks of winter.

You may want to include pictures of weather in action. If you have some old copies of *The Farmer's Almanac,* include these for students to look through.

2. Make a bulletin board of **Weather Records**. Everyone is interested in weather records. You'll find some on pages 32 and 33. Here are some others:

> U.S. highest temperature: 134°F on July 10, 1913, in Death Valley, California.
> Wadi Halfa, Sudan, had no rain in 19 years.
> Bahia Felix, Chile, has an average of 325 days of rain each year.
> U.S. lowest temperature: -76°F in January 1886, Tanana, Alaska.
> U.S. longest dry spell: 767 days (1912), in Bagdad, California.
> U.S. greatest 24-hour snowfall: 76 inches on April 14-15, 1921,
> in Silver Lake, Colorado.
> Longest lasting rainbow: 3 hours on August 14, 1979, in North Wales.

These records are more interesting when displayed with a world map showing the locations of the record holders.

3. Make cloud models. At the **Weather Center**, provide posterboard, scissors, glue, cotton, black tempera paint (powder), aluminum foil, string, black magic markers, and a cloud chart. Invite your students to make models of the main cloud types to hang from the ceiling. For a special effect, add a rainbow over a window or door.

4. At the **Weather Center**, provide materials to make each of the weather instruments (students can help collect these) so that they are on hand when they are needed. Laminate or cover a map of the United States with clear Contact paper. Use a wax pencil to mark the major fronts, high and low pressure areas, and types of precipitation. Post local weather information on the chalkboard. Have students update the map and predict the next day's weather.

5. Photocopy small maps of the United States. Make one for each day of the month. Use them instead of the plastic-coated map. Each day, date a new map, mark it for that day's weather, and add it to the bulletin board. This growing display will give students a chance to see how fronts, air masses, and areas of precipitation move across the country.

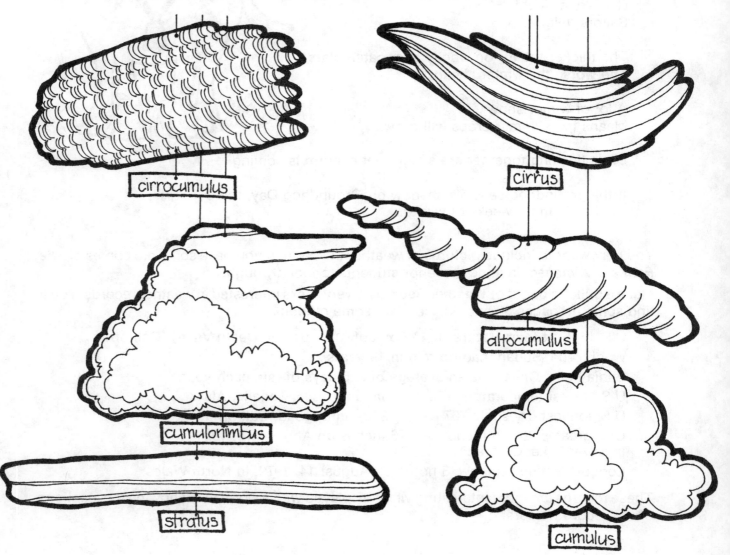

Name _____

PRETEST

Matching: Choose the best answer from the list of possible answers to complete each of the statements. Put the letter of your answer on the line in the statement.

A. winter   D. wind vane   G. hygrometer   J. cumulus
B. summer   E. rain gauge   H. nephoscope   K.
C. anemometer   F. barometer   I. cumulonimbus   L.

1. The earth receives the sun's rays less directly in the _____ .

2. A/An _____ is used to measure relative humidity.

3. A/An _____ is used to measure wind direction.

4. A/An _____ is used to measure wind speed.

5. A/An _____ is used to measure the amount of rainfall.

6. A/An _____ is used to measure the air pressure.

7. A/An _____ is used to observe the direction and speed of clouds.

8. _____ clouds usually mean fair weather.

9. _____ clouds usually mean thunderstorms.

10. A/An _____ is the weather map symbol for a cold front.

Short Answer: Write a short answer for each of these questions.

11. What is weather? _____

_____

_____

12. What is the Coriolis effect? _____

_____

_____

13. What is a prevailing wind? _____

_____

_____

Name _____

THE SUN'S HEAT, PART 1

Weather is the condition of the atmosphere with respect to heat or cold, wetness or dryness, calm or storm, and clearness or cloudiness. To understand weather, we measure temperature, the amount of moisture in the air, and the amount of rain or snowfall. We determine the speed and direction of the wind and observe the type and thickness of the clouds.

In observing weather, then, we are interested in air, heat, and water. In combination, these three things determine weather.

On the earth, heat is supplied by the sun. If we could set up a weather station on the sun, we would find that it is very hot. Why are there differences in temperature on the earth? Is there a difference in the way the earth receives the sun's heat?

The answer to this question is yes. The range in temperatures and the difference in the seasons is caused by the tilt of the earth. This investigation will help you understand why.

◼ Activity

Shine a flashlight straight down on a piece of paper from about six inches above. Outline the circle the light makes on the paper. Then, hold the flashlight the *same* distance from the paper, but from an angle. Again outline the circle the light makes. Which circle is smaller? Which circle is larger? In which circle was the light more concentrated? In which circle was the light more spread out, or diffuse?

In much the same way, the angle at which the sun's light and its heat strike the earth helps to determine how bright it is and how hot it feels.

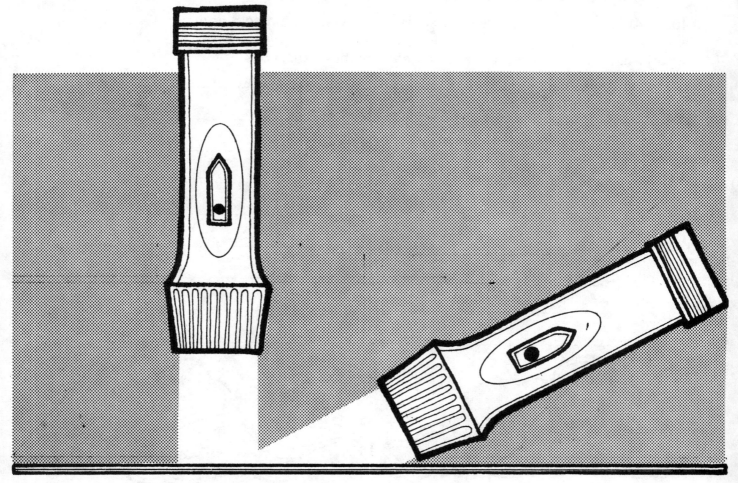

Name _____

THE SUN'S HEAT, PART 2

Even if the amount of sunlight is the same, temperatures may vary because masses of rock, soil, and dirt soak up heat differently.

Materials

three empty half-pint milk cartons
dark soil
light-colored sand
water
three Celsius thermometers

a heat lamp or sunny spot
a kitchen timer
a red pencil
a blue pencil

Instructions

1. Fill one carton with soil, one with sand, and one with water.
2. Put a thermometer in each carton so that the bulb is below the surface.

Activities

1. Place all three cartons under the heat lamp or in bright sunlight.

    a. Which one will get the warmest in fifteen minutes? _____

    _____

    b. Which one will hold the heat the longest? _____

    _____

2. Check the temperature every five minutes for fifteen minutes. Use the red pencil to make a line graph of the results.

3. Remove the cartons from the sun. Check the temperature every five minutes for another fifteen minutes. Use the blue pencil to record the results over the red line graphs.

    a. Which material got the warmest? _____

    b. Which material held the heat the longest? _____

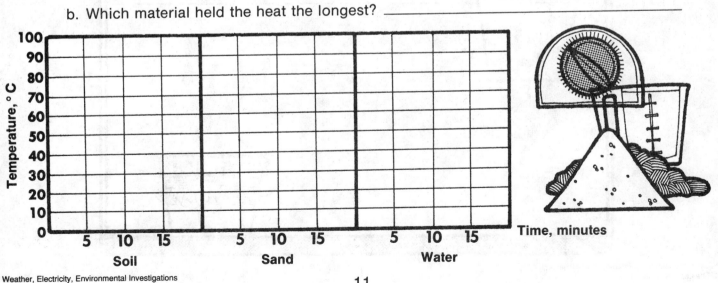

Name _____

WHAT MAKES THE WIND BLOW?

Air rises when it is heated and sinks when it is cooled. If you are not sure about that statement, feel the air directly above and below a lightbulb that has been on for at least ten minutes. Open a refrigerator door a crack and feel the air directly above and below the door.

Heated and cooled air is moving, but what happens to warm air and cool air when they meet? Because water and air are both fluids and react in the same way, we can experiment with water to see what would happen to air.

Materials

two styrofoam cups	a freezer	marbles	a pencil
red and blue food coloring	masking tape	a rubber band	water
clear plastic wrap	a fish tank		

Instructions

1. Fill one cup half full of water.
2. Add blue coloring to the water and place the cup in the freezer.
3. Fill the fish tank with lukewarm tap water.
4. When the water in the first cup is frozen, poke a hole in the bottom of the cup.
5. Tape the cup to the side of the fish tank with the hole below the surface of the water.
6. Fill the other cup with very hot water and add red coloring. Place marbles in the cup.
7. Cover the second cup with clear wrap. Use the rubber band to hold the wrap in place.
8. Place the cup of hot water on the bottom of the tank.
9. Once water in the tank becomes still, carefully poke a hole in the wrap with the pencil.

Activities

1. On a piece of paper, draw and color a picture to show what happened.
2. Tell what happened as the cold and warm fluids met.
3. Explain why this statement is true: *The sun makes the wind blow.*

Name _____

WHAT IS THE CORIOLIS EFFECT?

Away from ground level, wind blows because one large cold mass of air (called a **high pressure area**) moves toward and pushes under a large warm mass of air (called a **low pressure area**). If the earth was not spinning, the wind would always blow from the north if you lived north of the equator and from the south if you lived south of the equator; however, the turning of the earth has a very important effect on the wind. This effect is called the Coriolis effect. It is named after Gaspard Gustave de Coriolis (1792-1843), the French mathematician who first figured out why the wind did not blow strictly from the north or from the south.

Materials

a paper plate
scissors
a record player
a pencil

Instructions

1. Use the scissors to poke a hole through the center of the paper plate.
2. Put the plate on the turntable as you would a record.
3. Draw a straight line from the center spoke to the outside of the plate.
4. Turn on the record player and draw another straight line from the spoke to the outside.
5. Stop the record player and look at the second line you drew.

Activities

■ 1. On a piece of paper, explain what happened and why.
■ 2. Use an encyclopedia to find out if the earth is spinning clockwise or counterclockwise.

HOW TO MAKE AN ANEMOMETER

An **anemometer** measures wind speed. There are a number of different types of anemometers. The one described here is easy to make and to use.

Materials

30 cm of monofilament fishing line
a needle
a Ping-Pong ball
a protractor
clear tape
a piece of soft wood 1.25 cm x 1.25 cm x 20 cm
white glue

Instructions

1. Thread the needle with the monofilament line and poke a hole through the center of the Ping-Pong ball.
2. Knot the end of the thread and add a dab of glue to attach the line firmly to the ball.
3. Tape the free end of the line to the center of the straight edge of the protractor.
4. Use the glue to attach the piece of wood to the straight edge of the protractor as a handle. The handle helps keep your body movements from changing the reading.

■ Activity

To measure the wind speed, hold the anemometer by the handle and sight straight along the upper edge of the protractor. Keep the anemometer in this position while you check what angle the line is stretched across. Look up this angle measurement on the wind speed chart and record the corresponding speed. If the wind is gusting, take several readings and figure the average.

Wind Speed Chart

Angle, degrees	Wind Speed, mph	Angle, degrees	Wind Speed, mph
90°	0	50°	18.0
85°	5.8	45°	19.6
80°	8.2	40°	21.4
75°	10.1	35°	23.4
70°	11.8	30°	25.8
65°	13.4	25°	28.7
60°	14.9	20°	32.5
55°	16.4		

Name _____

HOW TO MAKE A WIND VANE

A **wind vane** is used to measure the direction of the wind near ground level. The most common direction of wind flow in the United States is from west to east; however, many local factors affect the direction of the wind.

Materials

plastic milk jug   a saw
scissors   two 5-cm nails
two tacks   a 6-cm length of stiff plastic tubing
one strip of soft wood 1.25 cm x 1.25 cm x 37 cm a hammer
a marking pen   two washers to fit over nails
a wood block about 10 cm square   a compass

Instructions

1. Cut an arrow head and tail from the sides of the milk jug.

2. Saw a slit in each end of the wood strip.
3. Insert the arrow head in one slit and the tail in the other.
4. Press a tack into the arrow head on one side of the wood strip.
5. Press a tack into the arrow tail on the opposite side of the wood strip.
6. Mark the center of the wood block.
7. Drive a nail from the bottom up through this center mark.
8. Label the top of the block with the main compass points.

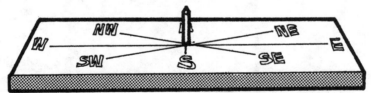

9. Carefully, drive a nail through the center of the wood strip an equal distance between the arrow head and tail.

10. Put a washer over the nail on the wood block.
11. Put the stiff tubing over the washer.
12. Put a washer over the nail on the arrow.
13. Insert the arrow nail into the tubing.

■ Activities

Each time you check wind direction, use a compass to point the base north, then see what direction the wind vane points.

Name _____

PREVAILING WINDS, PART 1

The most frequent or most common wind in a particular place or region is called the **prevailing wind**. It is named for the direction from which it blows.

Materials

a compass
your wind vane
your anemometer
a metric ruler
pencil
paper

Instructions

1. Make a dot in the center of your paper to stand for yourself.
2. Label the paper N, NE, E, SE, S, SW, W, and NW around the outer edge.
3. Go outside and find a place that is clear of any buildings or trees.
4. Use the compass to help you face north.
5. Use your wind vane and anemometer to find the wind direction and wind speed.

Activities

● 1. Draw a straight line on the paper toward the dot (you) to show what direction the wind was blowing from. Let every centimeter in length equal five miles per hour of wind speed.

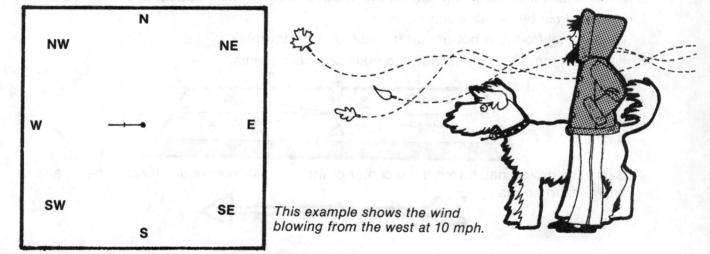

This example shows the wind blowing from the west at 10 mph.

■ 2. Go to the same place at the same time every day for one or two weeks (the longer the better) to check the wind direction and speed. Add a new line each day that the wind is blowing.

   a. From which direction did the wind blow most often? _____
      This is called the **prevailing wind**.

   b. From which direction did the strongest wind blow? _____

Name _____

PREVAILING WINDS, PART 2

A **wind rose** shows the wind speed and wind direction for a community over a period of time. A wind rose can be very helpful in planning community projects.

Activity

Pretend that you are a city commissioner for Hillville. It is your job to decide which of two proposed sites would make a better location for a city park. You also must decide whether a developer should be allowed to build a housing subdivision on the site proposed for that project. Use this wind rose for Hillville to help you make your choices.

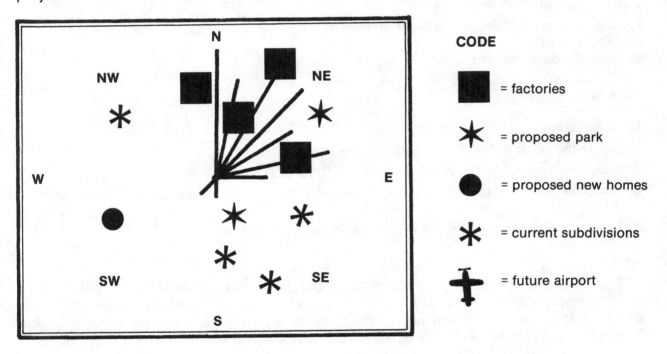

CODE

◼ = factories

✳ = proposed park

● = proposed new homes

✳ = current subdivisions

✈ = future airport

1. Which park site would you choose? _____

   Why did you make that choice? _____

   _____

2. Should the developer be allowed to build the new subdivision? _____

   Why or why not? _____

   _____

3. If, in the future, Hillville decided to build an airport, where would you suggest it be located?

   Add it to the diagram. Why did you pick this location? _____

   _____

   _____

Name _____

HOW TO MAKE A NEPHOSCOPE

Houses, trees, hills, and other man-made or natural objects can change the direction of the wind close to the ground, but have little or no affect on the winds high above the earth. A **meteorologist** (someone who studies the weather) uses gas-filled balloons and a special telescope to determine the direction of these winds. You can use a nephoscope. A **nephoscope** is used to observe the direction and speed of clouds and, thus, to indicate the direction of the wind high above the earth.

Materials

a small mirror
a sheet of white cardboard larger than the mirror
rubber cement
a small, round Band-Aid
a pen
a compass

Instructions

1. Cover the back of the mirror with rubber cement.
2. Attach the mirror to the middle of the cardboard.
3. Stick the Band-Aid to the center of the mirror. If necessary, cut the Band-Aid smaller so that it covers only a small part of the mirror.
4. Mark the compass directions around the outside of the mirror.

● Activity

Place the nephoscope on a flat surface outside. Use the compass to help you point the N on the nephoscope toward the north. Look for clouds in the mirror and follow one puff from the Band-Aid to the edge of the mirror. The direction the wind high above the earth is blowing from is exactly opposite the point where the cloud leaves the mirror.

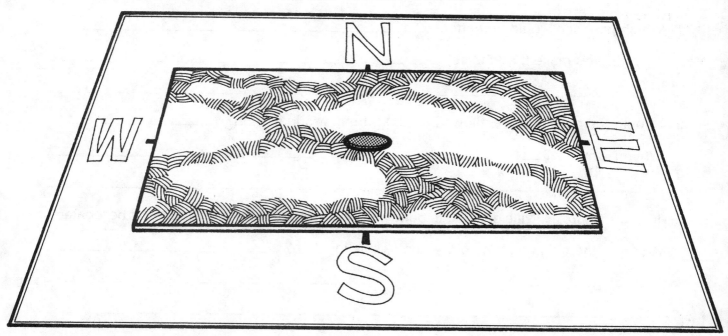

Name _____

THE CHILLING ADVENTURE

One day last fall, Tom, Fred, and Joe went for a walk in the woods. The trail was not well marked, and the boys became lost. Tom slipped and fell into a stream. Fred got wet pulling Tom out.

After a time, the boys realized that they had been walking in circles. Tired and discouraged, they decided to stay where they were and wait to be rescued.

They sat down side by side to wait. When the wind started to blow, Tom heaped leaves around himself in an effort to stay warm.

This investigation will help you to understand what the **wind chill factor** is and to see how it affected the three boys.

Materials

three thermometers   two pieces of cloth
a plastic bag with a tie   a kitchen timer

Instructions

1. Read and record the temperature on each thermometer.
2. Wet the pieces of cloth.
3. Put one piece of cloth over the bulb end of each of two thermometers. These represent Tom and Fred.
4. Put Tom's thermometer in the plastic bag and close the bag with the tie. (The bag represents the leaves.)
5. Place the dry bulb thermometer (represents Joe) next to the uncovered wet bulb thermometer.
6. Fan all three thermometers for two minutes.
7. Check and record the temperature on each thermometer.

Activities

■ 1. From your observations, answer these questions.
▲

    a. How does the wind affect body temperature? _____

    _____

    b. How does being wet affect body temperature? _____

    _____

    c. What effect would a nylon jacket or covering of leaves have? _____

    _____

    d. Why? _____

    _____

■ 2. Use a dictionary to look up the meaning of **wind chill factor**.

Name _____

LAND PUZZLES

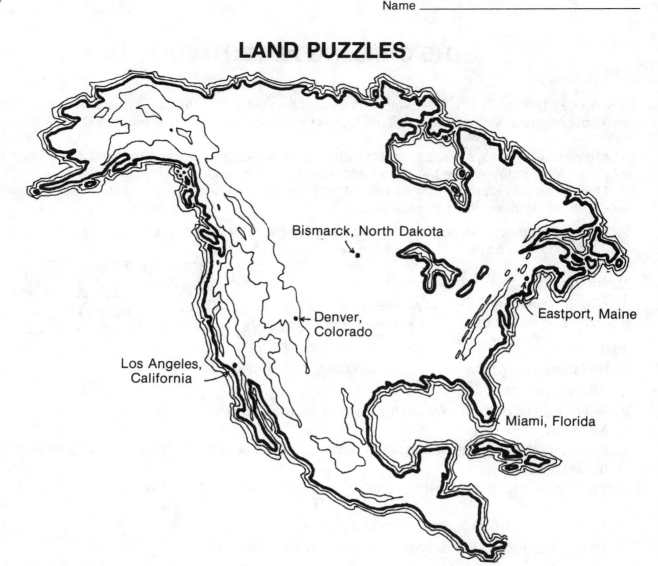

Bismarck, North Dakota

Denver, Colorado

Eastport, Maine

Los Angeles, California

Miami, Florida

Activities

1. Study this map. Then, solve the puzzles.

   a. This city gets most of its rain when the wind blows from the west. Easterly winds are usually dry. What city is it? _____

   b. It is colder in Bismarck than in Eastport in the winter. It is hotter in Bismarck than in Eastport in the summer. Both cities are equally far north. What makes the difference?

   _____

   _____

   c. Would a westerly wind be wet or dry in Denver? _____ Why? _____

   _____

★ 2. On the back of this page or on a separate piece of paper, list the geographic factors that affect the weather in your community.

Name _____

HOW TO MAKE A BAROMETER

The **barometer** is a very useful weather instrument because it measures a weather factor that we can neither see nor feel: the pressure of tiny air molecules. An increase in pressure means that the air is cooling. When the air is cool, the molecules move slower and are closer together. This condition is called **high pressure**. A decrease in pressure means that the air is warming. When the air is warm, the molecules move faster and are spread farther apart. This condition is called **low pressure**. A barometer makes us aware of these increases and decreases, which we may feel but cannot see.

Materials

a thermos bottle	white glue
a large rubber balloon	a large cereal box
scissors	a sheet of white paper
rubber bands	a metric ruler
a plastic straw	a pen

Instructions

1. Cut the balloon so that a piece of rubber can be stretched over the top of the thermos.
2. Use several rubber bands to hold this rubber piece in place.
3. Put a drop of glue in the center of the rubber piece.
4. Place one end of the straw in the glue.
5. Allow the glue to dry.
6. Glue the white paper to the center of one side of the box.
7. Mark the middle of the paper and label with the number 5.
8. Make five marks counting up and down from the 5, each 3 millimeters apart. Write the numbers 0 through 10 at the marks.
9. Place the box next to the thermos so that the straw normally points to the 5. If necessary, use books to adjust the height of the box or the thermos.

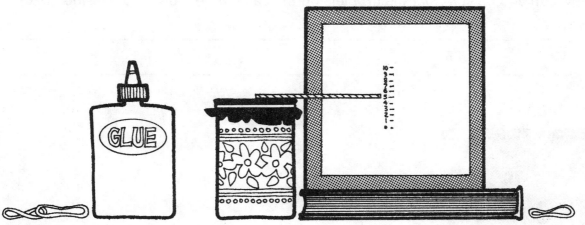

Activities

● 1. At several times during the week, take and record barometric readings.

■ 2. If possible, over a long period of time, correlate these readings with observed changes in the weather.

Name _____

WATER VAPOR

Water in the air is in the form of a gas. Water as a gas is called **water vapor**. Because the water molecules are fast moving and far apart, you cannot see water vapor. When water vapor condenses, the molecules slow down and move closer together to form water droplets, which you can see. In this investigation, you will be able to condense invisible water vapor into visible water droplets to prove that it is there.

Materials

an empty metal can with the label removed   a spoon
a thermometer   some ice
food coloring   water
salt

Instructions

1. Wash the can carefully inside and out.
2. Fill the can half full of water.
3. Add food coloring and salt to the water.
4. Stir well.
5. Put the thermometer into the water.
6. Add ice one cube at at time until droplets begin to form on the *outside* of the can.

Activity

Answer the following questions.

● 1. At what temperature did the droplets begin to form on the can?

  _____

■ 2. How can you be sure that the droplets on the can did not come from *inside* the can?

  _____

  _____

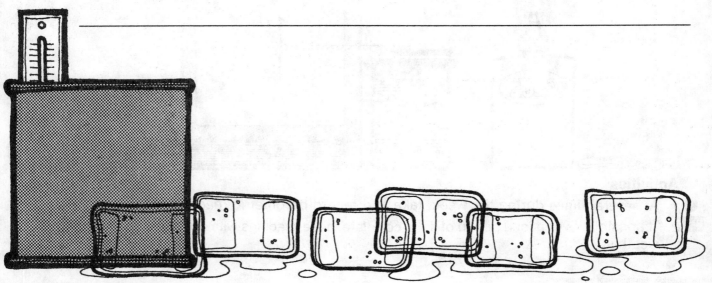

Name _____

WHERE WILL DEW FORM?

When water vapor in the air comes in contact with cooler objects or landforms, it condenses. We call the water droplets formed in this way **dew**.

Even if all of the objects left out overnight become equally cool, there is a chance that dew will not form on all of them. Try this investigation to find out what determines where dew will form.

Materials

five pieces of white paper
an umbrella
a yard with at least one tree

Instructions

1. On a clear, cool evening, put the pieces of paper outside at different locations: under the tree, under the open umbrella (prop the umbrella on one side), in the open, near the house, and on a walk or driveway.
2. Check all of the samples in the morning.
3. On the chart below, list where your samples were placed.
4. Put an X in the **Dew Found** box for each piece of paper that had at least some dew on it.
5. If you suspect that the water droplets soaked through the paper from the ground, repeat the experiment but put a piece of clear plastic wrap under each piece of paper.

Sample Locations	Dew Found
	☐
	☐
	☐
	☐
	☐

Activities

▲ 1. From your observations, formulate some hypotheses about where dew is most likely to form and why.

▲ 2. Devise some additional experiments you might conduct to test your hypotheses.

■ 3. Use a dictionary, encyclopedia, or science reference book to discover the relationship between **dew** and **frost**.

▲ 4. Based on what you have learned about the relationship between dew and frost, tell what steps farmers might take to prevent frost from damaging citrus fruits and other crops.

Name _____

HOW DO YOU MAKE A CLOUD?

Condensation occurs not only on objects on the ground, but also in the air. Water molecules come together to form water droplets. When these droplets collect around particles of dust and dirt in the air, a cloud forms.

Materials

a gallon jar
a large rubber balloon
scissors

rubber bands

wooden matches
a measuring cup
water

Instructions

1. Cut the neck off the balloon.
2. Put one-half cup of warm water into the gallon jar.
3. Cover the jar opening with the balloon rubber.
4. Wait several minutes. Then strike a match and blow it out. While the match is still smoking, quickly poke it inside the jar and catch the smoke.
5. Pull the balloon rubber back over the jar opening and secure it with the rubber bands.
6. Press down firmly on the center of the balloon rubber, count to five, and then pull up very quickly on the center of the rubber piece. If the cloud is hard to see, repeat this procedure in a dark room while someone shines a flashlight at the jar.

◼ Activity

Complete the recipe for making a cloud.

To make one cloud, mix _____ and _____ .

Then _____ until the

_____ condenses.

Name _____

CLOUDS CAN HELP PREDICT THE WEATHER

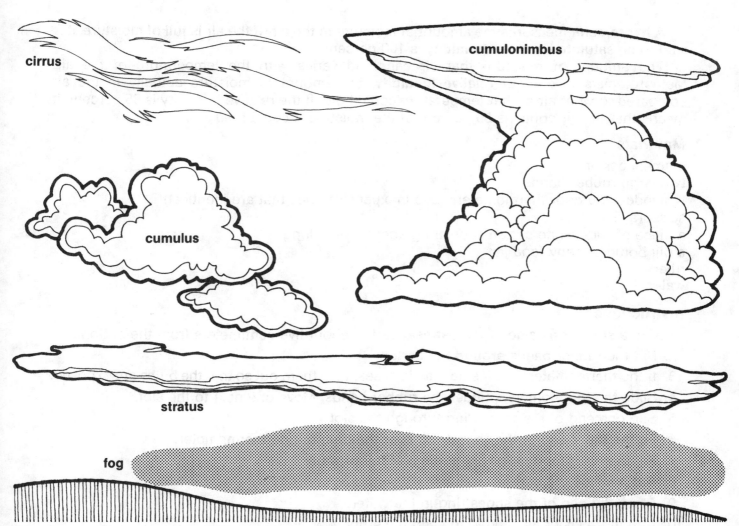

When water vapor (water in the form of a gas) condenses in the air, various types of clouds form.

fog   Clouds close to the ground. Fog often forms when cold air settles to the ground on a clear, windless night.

stratus   Gray sheets of clouds that usually mean slow, steady rain or snow.

cumulus   Puffy fair weather clouds that are caused by rising warm air.

cumulonimbus   Fast rising clouds with a spreading top. These clouds usually mean thunderstorms and strong winds.

cirrus   Clouds made of ice crystals which are found five miles or higher above the earth. Cirrus clouds go with fair weather; but when they spread across the sky, a weather change is coming.

◼ Activity

For two weeks, keep a chart showing the kinds of clouds you see and the weather for each day.

Name _____

HOW TO MAKE A HYGROMETER

A **hygrometer** measures the amount of moisture in the air. If the air is full of moisture, it is said to be saturated and the **humidity** is 100 percent.

The amount of moisture that air can hold varies with the temperature of the air. Meteorologists talk about **relative humidity**, the amount of moisture actually in the air compared to what air at that temperature could hold. If the relative humidity is 55 percent, it means that the air contains 55 percent of the moisture it could hold.

Materials

oatmeal carton
two large rubber bands
two indoor/outdoor thermometers (use inexpensive ones that are identical)
scissors
a piece of wide white cotton shoestring about 15 cm long
a pill bottle or baby food jar
ruler
water

Instructions

1. Cut a slot in one side of the oatmeal carton about five centimeters from the bottom.
2. Put the rubber bands around the carton.
3. If the thermometers are inside plastic cases, take them out so that the bulbs are exposed.
4. Slide the thermometers under the rubber bands. Move one next to the slot.
5. Slip one end of the shoestring through the slot.
6. Fit the other end of the shoestring over the bulb of one thermometer.
7. Fill the baby food jar or pill bottle half full of water.
8. Put it inside the carton.
9. Place the end of the shoestring in the water.
10. Add more water as needed to keep the string wet.

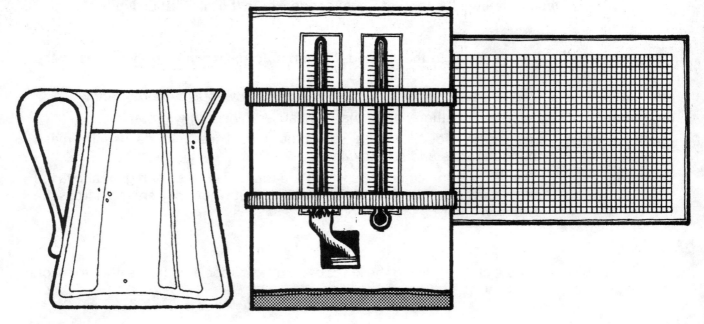

Name ____________________

HOW TO USE YOUR HYGROMETER

To calculate the relative humidity, read the dry bulb and the wet bulb thermometers. Subtract the wet bulb reading from the dry bulb reading. Then use this chart to find the percent of relative humidity.

Dry Bulb Temperature, °C

Difference Between Dry Bulb and Wet Bulb Temperature, °C

	5	6	7	8	9	10	11	12	13	14	15	16	17	18	19	20	21	22	23	24
1	86	86	87	87	88	88	89	89	90	90	90	90	90	91	91	91	92	92	92	92
2	72	73	74	75	76	77	78	78	79	79	80	81	81	82	82	83	83	83	84	84
3	58	60	62	63	64	66	67	68	69	70	71	71	72	73	74	74	75	76	76	77
4	45	48	50	51	53	55	56	58	59	60	61	63	64	65	65	66	67	68	69	69
5	33	35	38	40	42	44	46	48	50	51	53	54	55	57	58	59	60	61	62	62
6	20	24	26	29	32	34	36	39	41	42	44	46	47	49	50	51	53	54	55	56
7	7	11	15	19	22	24	27	29	32	34	36	38	40	41	43	44	46	47	48	49
8				8	12	15	18	21	23	26	27	30	32	34	36	37	39	40	42	43
9						6	9	12	15	18	20	23	25	27	29	31	32	34	36	37
10									7	10	13	15	18	20	22	24	26	28	30	31
11											6	8	11	14	16	18	20	22	24	26
12														7	10	12	14	17	19	20

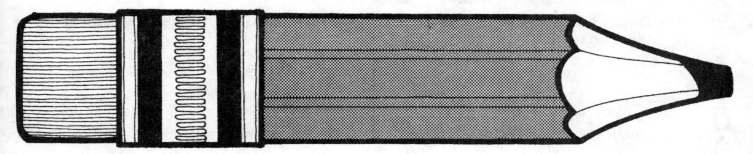

Activities

■ 1. For three days, check the relative humidity outside in the morning and again in the afternoon. Make a bar graph to show the results.

■ 2. What time of day was the relative humidity higher, morning or afternoon? ____________

▲ Why? ____

____

▲ 3. What will happen if the relative humidity is close to 100 percent? ____________

____

Name _____

HOW TO MAKE A RAIN GAUGE

A **rain gauge** is a weather instrument used to measure rainfall. Rainfall is measured in inches. It is common to measure rainfall in as small a measurement as a hundredth of an inch if very little falls.

Materials

a funnel
a jar with a mouth on which the funnel can rest
a ruler marked off in inches
masking tape and a black permanent marking pen

Instructions

1. To make a simple rain gauge, rest the funnel in the mouth of the jar.
2. Stick a strip of masking tape to the outside of the jar and mark off inch increments on it with the marking pen.
3. Put the rain gauge outside so that it is in the open away from buildings and trees.

Activities

1. To find out how much rain has fallen, figure out the ratio between the diameter of the funnel and the diameter of the can or jar.

   a. Measure the diameter of each. The diameter is the distance across the open top.

   Funnel diameter = _____

   Can or jar diameter = _____

   b. Divide each of these measurements in half to find the radius (one-half the distance across the open top).

   Funnel radius = _____

   Can or jar radius = _____

   c. Find the square of the radius by multiplying the radius times itself.

   Square of funnel radius = _____

   Square of can or jar radius = _____

   d. Use the squares of these measurements as the ratio for comparing collected water to the actual rainfall. If the square of the funnel radius is 9 and the square of the container radius is 1, the ratio is 9 to 1. By that ratio, every 9 inches of collected rain would equal 1 inch of actual rainfall.

2. Compare rainfall statistics from several parts of your state, the United States, or the world. How do the rainfall differences you observe affect the natural vegetation in these areas and the ways in which people live and earn their living?

3. How might a drastic change in the amount of rainfall where you live affect your family and you?

Name _____

WHAT DOES A WEATHER MAP TELL YOU? PART 1

Symbols are used on weather maps to show current weather information. By seeing where high and low pressure air masses are located (high pressure areas move toward low pressure areas) and checking wind directions and speed, meteorologists can predict future weather conditions.

Fronts are the boundaries between two different air masses.

 Cold front. Cold air pushes up warm air. A thunderstorm is usually followed by cooler, clear weather.

Warm front. Warm air slowly pushes out cold air. Slow, steady rain followed by warm, damp weather.

 Stationary front. Warm air and cool air meet, but neither moves out of the way.

Occluded front. Three air masses are involved. A warm air mass is trapped between a cold air mass on the ground and a higher cold air mass.

The words HIGH and LOW on the map tell where the center of the air mass is located. Next to the name of each city, a circle shows some special information about the weather in that community. These circle codes may vary slightly.

| clear | partly cloudy | overcast | rain | snow |

CLOUD SYMBOLS

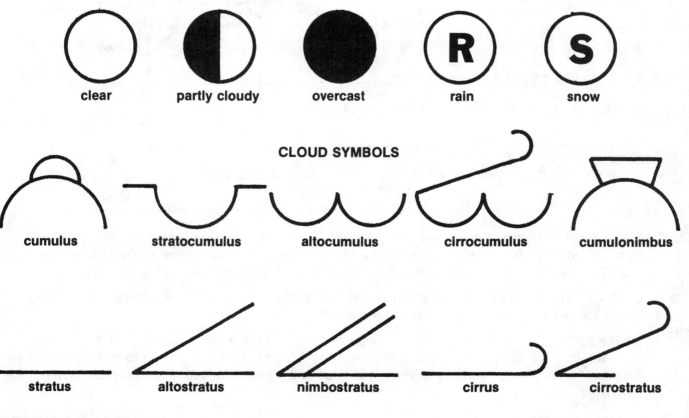

| cumulus | stratocumulus | altocumulus | cirrocumulus | cumulonimbus |

| stratus | altostratus | nimbostratus | cirrus | cirrostratus |

Name _____

WHAT DOES A WEATHER MAP TELL YOU? PART 2

Shaded areas show where precipitation (rain, snow, sleet, or hail) is falling. Flags next to the city name show the wind speed. The stick of the flag points in the direction from which the wind is blowing. The first number by the flag shows the temperature in degrees Fahrenheit. The second number, if there is one, shows the amount of rainfall in inches in the past six hours.

Activities

1. Use this sample weather map to answer the questions.

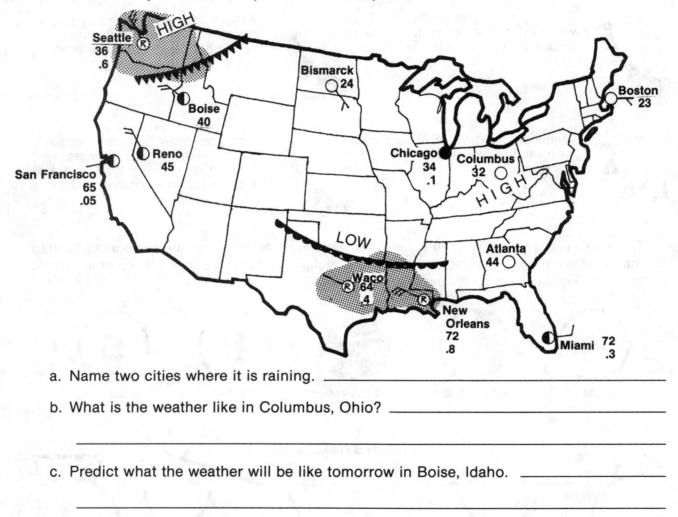

a. Name two cities where it is raining. _____

b. What is the weather like in Columbus, Ohio? _____

_____

c. Predict what the weather will be like tomorrow in Boise, Idaho. _____

_____

2. Make a two-column chart on which you list in one column groups of people to whom weather and accurate weather prediction is important and tell in the other column how weather affects them and why accurate prediction of it is important to them.

3. Compare the weather in several coastal cities. What similarities and differences do you notice? What factors might account for these?

4. Over a period of time, keep track of the weather predictions made for an area and the actual weather in that area. How accurate were the predictions? If weather predictions are inaccurate, what value do they have? Would you call meteorology an exact science? Why or why not?

Name _____

MAKING YOUR OWN WEATHER FORECASTS

■
▲ Use the weather instruments you have made to collect weather data for one week. Check your instruments at the same time every morning. Record your data on the chart. In the forecast
✱ section, make your prediction for that day's weather.
■

Weather Chart

Time of daily check _____

Date	Barometric Reading (Rising, falling, steady)	Temperature	Relative Humidity	Wind Speed	Wind Direction	Sky ◯ ◑ ●	Forecast
						◯	
						◯	
						◯	
						◯	
						◯	
						◯	
						◯	

Name _____

WEATHER RECORDS, PART 1

People are always trying to set records. Over the years, the weather has set some very impressive records of its own.

world's highest surface wind speed	231 mph on April 12, 1934, in Mt. Washington, New Hampshire
world's windiest place	Commonwealth Bay, George V Coast, Antarctica, with gales of 200 mph
world's most intense rainfall	1.50 inches in one minute on November 26, 1970, in Barst, Guadeloupe
largest officially reported hailstone	1.67 pounds (7½ inches in diameter) on September 3, 1970, in Coffeyville, Kansas
world's lowest temperature	-125°F on August 25, 1958, in Vostok, Antarctica
world's highest temperature	136°F on September 13, 1922, in El Azizia, Libya
U.S. greatest two-minute temperature rise	49°F (from -4°F to 45°F) on January 22, 1943, in Spearfish, South Dakota

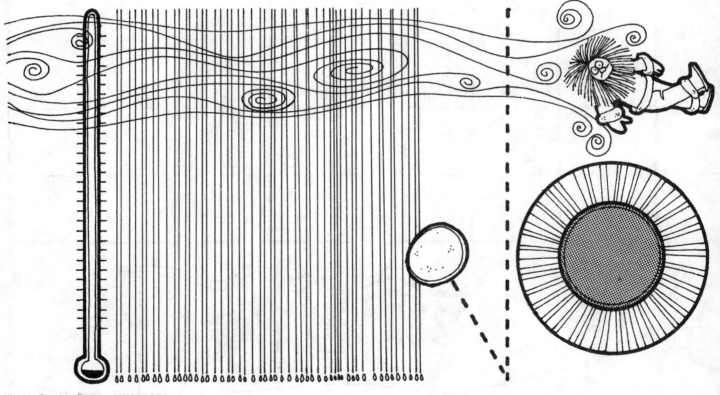

Name _____

WEATHER RECORDS, PART 2

Activities

■ 1. Write a story about what it might be like to find the world's largest hailstone.

▲ 2. Make a papier-mâché model (in correct size and weight) of the Coffeyville hailstone.

▲ 3. Write a poem about being on Mt. Washington on April 12, 1934, during the time that the world's highest surface wind was blowing.

■ 4. Try to find out the weather records for your community. Make a poster about these events.

▲ 5. Write a story about Spearfish, South Dakota, the day the temperature leaped up forty-nine degrees in two minutes.

▲ 6. Write an eyewitness account or an interview with someone who was in Barst, Guadeloupe, on November 26, 1970, when it rained 1.50 inches in one minute.

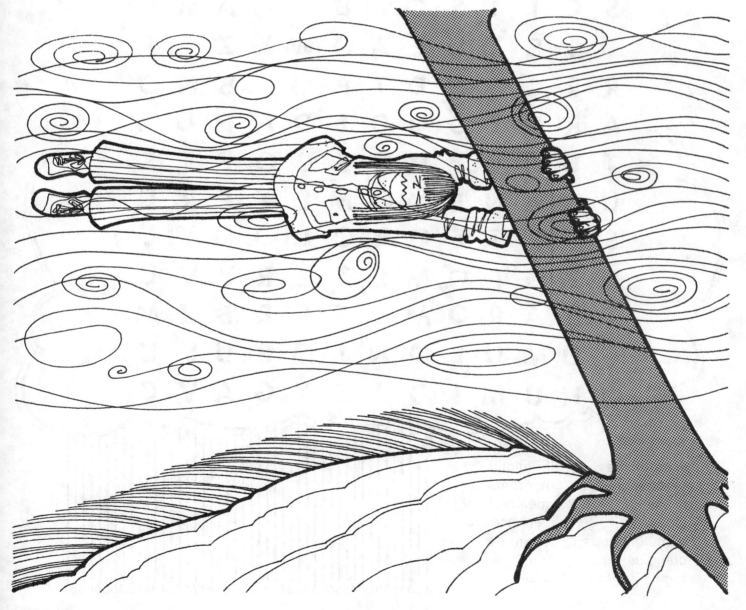

Name _____

WEATHER BRAIN BUSTERS

●   Find the fourteen weather words in this puzzle. The words may be written horizontally, vertically, diagonally, or even backwards. As you find the words, check them off in the list below.

■   Use these words and their definitions to make your own crossword puzzle. Paste your puzzle on a piece of cardboard and cover it with clear Contact paper. Supply a friend with a grease pencil and challenge him or her to work your puzzle. Wipe the puzzle clean when your friend has finished and pass it on to someone else.

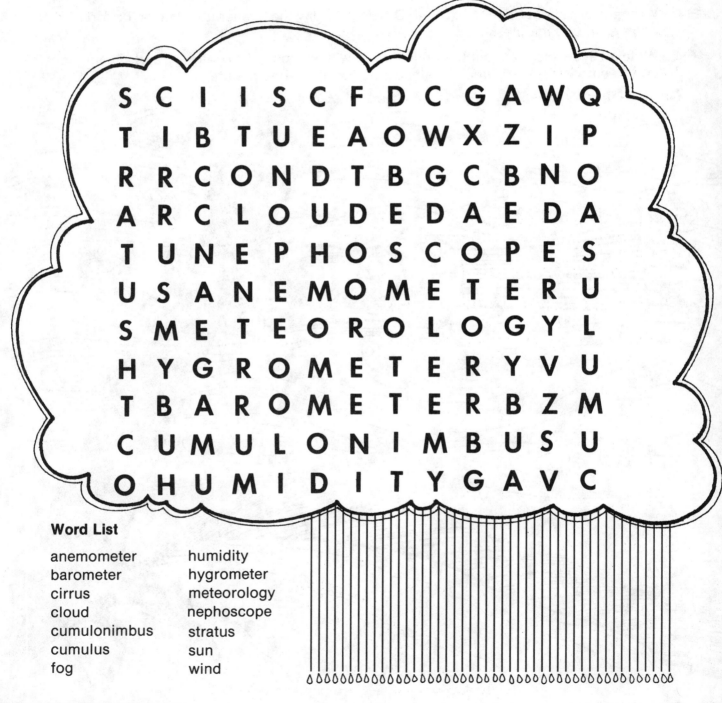

```
S C I I S C F D C G A W Q
T I B T U E A O W X Z I P
R R C O N D T B G C B N O
A R C L O U D E D A E D A
T U N E P H O S C O P E S
U S A N E M O M E T E R U
S M E T E O R O L O G Y L
H Y G R O M E T E R Y V U
T B A R O M E T E R B Z M
C U M U L O N I M B U S U
O H U M I D I T Y G A V C
```

Word List

anemometer   humidity
barometer   hygrometer
cirrus   meteorology
cloud   nephoscope
cumulonimbus   stratus
cumulus   sun
fog   wind

ADDITIONAL INFORMATON SOURCES
and
CORRELATED ACTIVITIES

Additional Sources

Feravolo, Rocco V. *Weather Experiments.* New York: Garrard, 1963.

Forsdyke, A. G. *Weather and Weather Forecasting.* New York: Grosset & Dunlap, 1970.

Ross, Frank, Jr. *Weather: From Ancient Times to the Space Age.* New York: Lothrop, 1964.

Zim, Herbert S. *Weather.* Racine, Wis.: Western Publishing.

Correlated Activities

1. For a list of the weather booklets, charts, and maps that are available free of charge or for a small fee, write to:

   > Superintendent of Documents
   > U.S. Government Printing Office
   > Washington, D.C. 20402

2. Invite a local meteorologist to visit your class. Discuss job responsibilities and the academic preparation required for this career.

3. Visit a local weather station.

4. Write an original radio play about a weather event complete with sound effects.

5. Describe and analyze ways in which the eruption of a volcano could affect the weather nearby or in a more distant region.

6. Some meteorologists believe that the earth is headed toward another ice age. Find and compare arguments for and against this theory.

7. Look up information about how satellites are used to forecast storms. Report your findings to the class.

8. Discover what causes lightning and thunder. Explain these weather phenomena to the class.

9. Find out about the nitrogen cycle and explain how lightning affects plant growth.

10. What is a tornado? What is a hurricane? In what ways are they the same? In what ways are they different?

11. Make a chart showing the damage caused by tornadoes in a particular part of the country or during a particular time period.

12. Divide the class into weather teams. Have each team construct a set of the weather instruments. Assign each team a specific area on the school grounds in which to take regular weather readings. Select locations that have different exposures. Some should have wind breaks while others should be in the open. Mark these spots in some way. Allow time each morning for readings to be taken and recorded. Have a display area where each team can list its daily weather data and make its daily forecast. If possible, include graphs and photographs in the display. Have the team members list and discuss all of the factors that influence the readings at their stations.

13. Select a wide-mouthed can. (The opening must be as large as the can bottom.) Place a strip of tape on the outside of the can. Mark inches and half inches on the tape. Place the can outside when snow is expected. After snow falls, measure the snow collected in the can.

14. Go for a snow drift walk. Use a yardstick to measure each drift. If a camera is available, take pictures of the drifts. List what each drift formed against. Can you tell by looking at a drift which direction the wind was blowing? Try to decide why the drift has its particular shape. Why do some drifts have an overhanging curl? What factors affect the way snow drifts?

15. Scoop up ten inches of snow with your marked can. Let the snow melt. How many inches of water are left? (Normally, ten inches of snow equals one inch of water; however, some snows are wetter than others.)

16. Collect two cups of snow right after the snow stops or while it is still snowing. Let the snow melt. Put a paper towel over a clean glass. Pour the snow water through the towel into the glass. How clean is the towel after the water has been poured through it? Repeat this test after the snow has been on the ground for several days. Compare your results and offer at least one possible explanation for the difference you observe.

Name _____

POSTTEST

Matching: Which kind of weather instrument would you use to collect data on each of these weather factors? Choose your answer from the list and write the corresponding letter on the line.

A. nephoscope   C. hygrometer   E. rain gauge
B. anemometer   D. wind vane   F. barometer

1. Wind speed   _____
2. Wind direction high
   above the earth   _____
3. Relative humidity   _____
4. Wind direction at
   ground level   _____
5. Rainfall   _____
6. Air pressure   _____

Correcting: Each of these statements is false. Cross out the part that is incorrect and print above it the word or words that would make it correct.

7. Cumulus clouds usually mean thunderstorms.

8. A meteorologist studies meteors and asteroids.

9. When it is windy, the air feels warmer.

10. The relative humidity is the amount of water it takes to make a cloud.

11. A high pressure area is warm air.

12. Choose one of the following topics to write about.

   a. Explain how to make a wind rose for your community and why a wind rose is important in community planning.

   b. Explain how the sun causes the wind to blow.

ANSWERS

Page 9, Pretest
1. A 2. G 3. D 4. C 5. E. 6. F 7. H 8. J 9. I 10. K 11. Weather is the condition of the atmosphere with respect to heat or cold, wetness or dryness, calm or storm, and clearness or cloudiness. 12. The motion of the winds to the right in the Northern Hemisphere and to the left in the Southern Hemisphere as a result of the earth's rotation. 13. The most frequent wind in a particular place or region. It is named for the direction from which it blows.

Page 10, The Sun's Heat, Part 1
When the flashlight is directly above the paper, the area of light will be smaller and brighter.

Page 11, The Sun's Heat, Part 2
1a.b. Answers will vary. 3a. The dirt will become the warmest. b. The water will hold its heat the longest.

Page 12, What Makes the Wind Blow?
2. As the cold and warm fluids met, cool and warm currents swirled and mixed. The cool current pushed under the warm. 3. The sun makes the wind blow because it heats areas differently. Air moves from cooler to warmer areas. This air movement is what we call wind. The greater the difference in heating or temperature, the more rapid the air movement and the stronger the wind.

Page 13, What Is the Coriolis Effect?
1. The line drawn while the turntable was spinning is curved. 2. The earth spins counterclockwise.

Page 16, Prevailing Winds, Part 1
Answers will vary.

Page 17, Prevailing Winds, Part 2
1. The site to the northeast. This area will be relatively free of factory pollution. 2. No. This area lies in the path of noise and airborne pollution. 3. The airport could be built to the north, the northeast, or the east beyond the factories, or it could be built to the west. Any of these sites would be away from present housing areas and relatively free of the airborne pollutants that could affect visibility.

Page 19, The Chilling Adventure
a. If all other things are equal, wind will lower body temperature faster than still air of the same temperature. b. Being wet will cause the body to cool faster than if it were dry. c. A nylon jacket or covering of leaves helps to prevent cooling. d. Because it protects the body from the wind and may trap layers of air which serve to insulate the body and prevent heat loss.

Page 20, Land Puzzles
1a. Los Angeles b. Eastport's weather is moderated by the ocean. c. Dry. The mountains block rain from the west.

Page 22, Water Vapor
1. The dew point will vary depending on environmental conditions. 2. The water droplets on the can are uncolored and unsalted.

Page 23, Where Will Dew Form?
The papers that are covered are not likely to show any dew.

Page 24, How Do You Make a Cloud?
To make one cloud, mix water vapor and dust. Then cool or compress until the water vapor condenses.

Page 27, How to Use Your Hygrometer
2. The relative humidity will usually be higher in the morning because the air is cooler then, and when the air is cooler, it cannot hold as much moisture. 3. When the relative humidity is close to 100 percent, there will be some precipitation.

Page 29-30, What Does a Weather Map Tell You?
1. It is raining in Seattle, Waco, and New Orleans. 2. It is cold and clear in Columbus, and no wind is blowing. 3. It will be rainy and colder tomorrow in Boise as the cold front moves in.

Page 31, Making Your Own Weather Forecasts
Answers will vary.

Weather

Page 34, Weather Brain Busters

```
S C I I S C F D C G A W Q
T I B T U E A Q W X Z I P
R R C O N D T B G C B N O
A R C L O U D E D A E D A
T U N E P H O S C O P E S
U S A N E M O M E T E R U
S M E T E O R O L O G Y L
H Y G R O M E T E R Y V U
T B A R O M E T E R B Z M
C U M U L O N I M B U S U
O H U M I D I T Y G A V C
```

Page 38, Posttest

1. B 2. A 3. C 4. D 5. E 6. F 7. Cumulonimbus clouds usually mean thunderstorms or Cumulus clouds usually mean fair weather. 8. An astronomer studies meteors and asteroids or A meteorologist studies the weather. 9. When it is windy, the air feels cooler. 10. The relative humidity is the amount of water in the air compared to the amount it can hold. 11. A high pressure area is cool air or A low pressure area is warm air. 12a. A wind rose is made by recording the wind speed and direction over a period of time to determine the prevailing winds. Information obtained in this way makes it possible to locate housing tracts away from factory noise and out of the path of airborne pollution. 12b. The sun heats areas differently. Cooler air moves toward and under warmer air. This mixing of air is called wind. The greater the temperature difference, the more violent the mixing and the stronger the wind.

DEW   HURRICANE   SMOG
RAIN   LIGHTNING
CLOUDS   FOG   SLEET
BREEZE   WIND
THUNDER   MIST
HAIL   SNOW   ICE
FROST   TORNADO   HUMIDITY

_____
(name of student)

has successfully completed a unit of study

on

Weather

and has been named

a

Magnificent Meteorologist

at

_____
(name of school)

_____
(date)

_____
(signature of teacher)

BULLETIN BOARD AND LEARNING CENTER IDEAS

1. Have your students make a **paper chain** and write on each link the name of one thing that uses electricity. Add a paper plug to the end of the chain and show it connected to a super-sized wall outlet.

2. Set up a **static tester**. Use a big cardboard box with one side cut open. Inside, from the top of the box, suspend a variety of lightweight objects that might be attracted by another object with a static charge. The suspended objects should be about twelve to fifteen centimeters apart. With string, attach several balloons to the outside of the box and provide a piece of wool cloth for generating a static charge on the balloons. Challenge students to find out which objects are attracted to a static charge and which are not.

3. At a **Power Center**, provide D-cell batteries, flashlight bulbs, short pieces of insulated copper wire, scissors, and electrician's tape. Challenge students to devise a system that will make one bulb light, two bulbs light, or three bulbs light. Students will discover a great deal about circuits through simple manipulation.

4. Label a bulletin board **Power On**. On it, display pictures of anything that runs on electricity. Invite your students to add to this display. At the **Power Center**, provide magazines, construction paper, scissors, and glue. Suggest that students make montages with pictures of items that operate on battery power.

5. Set up a class experiment to determine which battery lasts the longest. Use three *identical* flashlights powered by three *different* types of batteries. If the flashlights have been used previously, put new bulbs in all three before you begin. Turn off all three flashlights while the class is out of the room so that everyone will be present when the first flashlight goes off. Use a bar graph to keep track of the number of hours each flashlight continues to shine.

6. Supply materials at the **Power On** center for students to make posters about conserving electricity. These could be put up around the school. Smaller posters could go home as reminders to turn off lights, keep refrigerator doors closed, and use less hot water.

7. Write each event named below on a separate card. Make these cards available at the **Power On** center. Challenge students to find out when each of these events took place and to make a time line of the development of electricity.

A. Thales found that amber attracted some things.
B. Otto von Guericke generated static electricity with a friction machine.
C. Charles François Du Fay found there were two kinds of electric charges, positive and negative.
D. Pieter van Musschenbroek discovered the principle of the Leyden jar, the earliest form of electrical condenser.
E. Benjamin Franklin proved lightning was electricity and invented the lightning rod.
F. Alessandro Volta invented the battery.
G. Michael Faraday made the first generator.
H. Joseph Henry made the first electric motor.
I. Samuel F. B. Morse invented the telegraph.
J. Alexander Graham Bell developed the telephone.
K. Thomas Alva Edison invented the incandescent electric lamp.

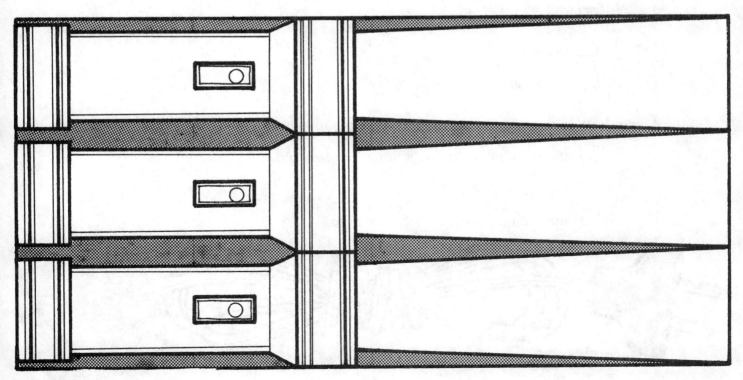

Name _____

PRETEST

Put an **X** in the box next to each phrase that best completes the statement.

1. Electricity is

   ☐ particles of power bouncing around in wires.

   ☐ electrons flowing from one place to another.

   ☐ sparks flowing from one place to another.

2. A short circuit happens

   ☐ when the current follows the easiest path.

   ☐ when the circuit is six centimeters or less in length.

   ☐ when the circuit is broken.

3. An example of a good conductor of electricity is

   ☐ a rubber band.

   ☐ a steel paper clip.

   ☐ a piece of glass.

4. When some of the electricity goes to each light bulb, the bulbs are said to be connected

   ☐ incompletely.

   ☐ in parallel.

   ☐ in series.

5. A light bulb is called an incandescent light because

   ☐ the filament inside gets hot enough to glow.

   ☐ the glass glows.

   ☐ the light is canned inside the bulb.

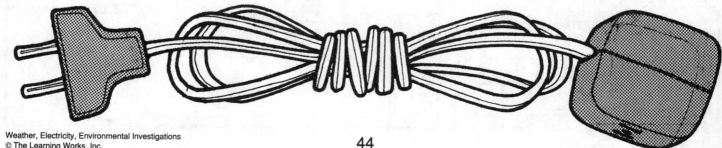

Name _____

THE POWER OF THE YELLOW STONE

The name **electricity** goes back to ancient Greece and the experiments of a wise man named Thales. Thales found a yellow, glassy stone. When he rubbed the stone between his fingers, he noticed that it attracted some threads on his clothes. We call this stone **amber**. In Greek, it was called *elektron.*

Friction made an electric charge build up on the surface of the stone. Friction can also cause an electric charge to build up on the surface of your body. This charge is called **static electricity**. It can be strong enough to make a spark and give you quite a jolt.

■ Activity

Write about one very shocking experience you have had with static electricity.

Name _____

WHAT IS ELECTRICITY?

Everything is made up of **atoms**. **Electrons** are tiny particles orbiting the nucleus of an atom. Different kinds of atoms have different numbers of electrons. When these electrons are knocked loose, they go zipping off on their own. These free-flying electrons are electricity. **Friction**, or rubbing, is one way to free electrons.

The term **static electricity** is used to mean any electricity that is not flowing through a wire or a conductor, but it is not really a good term. **Static** means "not moving," and all electricity is moving. **Electricity** is electrons flowing from one place to another.

Activities

● 1. Rub a balloon against a piece of wool cloth or a wool sweater. Then, hold it close to your hair. What happens?

_____

_____

● 2. Rub the balloon against the wool again. Hold the balloon up to a wall and let go. What happens?

_____

_____

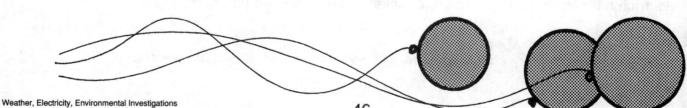

Name _____

WHICH CHARGE IS IT? PART 1

In 1733, a Frenchman named Charles François Du Fay made a number of experiments to see how charged objects would react to one another. He proved that objects may have only two kinds of charges. We call these charges **positive** and **negative**.

This investigation shows how two charged objects react, and it shows how a charge may travel and still have an effect.

Materials

aluminum foil
scissors
masking tape
an empty metal can (label removed)
two blocks of paraffin
a balloon
a piece of wool cloth
ruler

Instructions

1. Cut one long strip of aluminum foil about thirty centimeters long and about five centimeters wide.

2. Cut two short strips of foil each about fifteen centimeters long and five centimeters wide.

3. Place the can on top of a block of paraffin on a table top.

4. Put the other paraffin block at the edge of the table.

5. Tape one end of the long foil strip to the side of the can.

6. Move the can and wax block close to the table edge.

7. Tape the free end of the strip to the other wax block.

8. Tape the two short foil strips to the wax block so that they touch the end of the long strip. The two short strips should hang over the side of the table.

9. Rub the inflated balloon with the wool cloth. Make between twenty and fifty strokes in one direction only.

10. Touch the balloon to the can.

Name _____

WHICH CHARGE IS IT? PART 2

Activities

1. Observe what happens and answer the questions.

a. What happened to the two short strips? _____

   _____

b. In this experiment, the charge moves to four different places. List these four places in order.

   _____

   _____

   _____

   _____

2. Charles François Du Fay discovered these three facts about charged and uncharged objects:

   • Objects with the same charge push away from each other.
   • Objects with different charges attract each other.
   • A charged object attracts an uncharged object.

   This knowledge created a problem. When Charles Du Fay held a feather close to a piece of yarn, the two objects moved together. He didn't know if that meant that the feather and the yarn had different charges or if only one object was charged. How could he find out if both objects were charged?

   _____

   _____

   _____

   _____

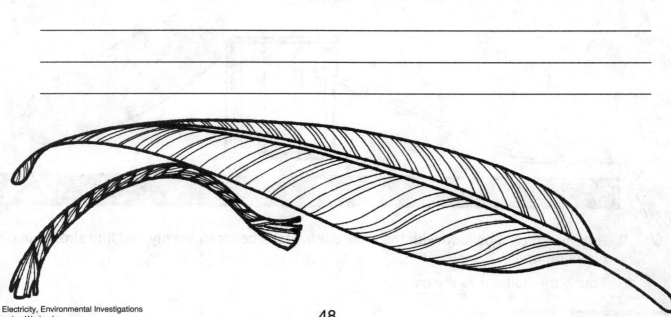

Name _____

CAN A MAGNET GENERATE AN ELECTRIC CURRENT?
PART 1

   When an electric charge moves from one place to another, this movement is called **electric current**. Some currents are very weak, while others are strong.
   First, make this **electric meter** so that you will be able to observe the movement of even a weak current. Then, use your electric meter to determine the results of this investigation.

Materials
five meters of thin, insulated copper wire
a small, cylindrical cardboard carton (such as oatmeal or salt comes in)
scissors
electrician's tape
a shoe box with a lid
a compass
one D-cell battery

Instructions
1. Cut open the bottom of the carton.

2. Wind the wire in tight coils around the carton. Leave thirty centimeters of wire free at each end.

3. Lay a strip of electrician's tape over the coils to hold them in place.

4. Trim the carton to remove extra cardboard.

5. Strip the insulation from each end of the wire.

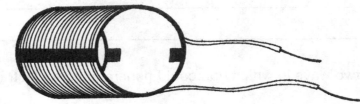

6. Place the coil in the shoe box.

7. Cut a section of the shoe box lid to fit through the middle of the coil.

8. Place the compass on this shelf.

9. Rotate the compass until the needle points to the center of the coil on each side.

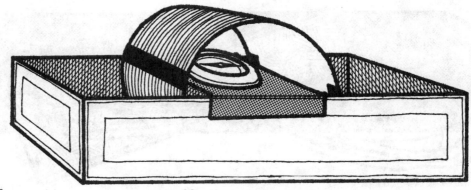

Name _____

CAN A MAGNET GENERATE AN ELECTRIC CURRENT?
PART 2

■ **Activity**

Touch one of the bare wire ends to each end of the D-cell battery. How does the compass react?

_____

_____

Materials

five meters of thin, insulated copper wire
an empty cardboard paper towel tube
a strong bar magnet
ruler

Instructions

1. Wrap the wire in tight coils around the cardboard tube leaving thirty centimeters free at each end.

2. Strip the insulation from each end of the wire.

3. Twist the bare wire ends of the coil onto the bare wire ends of the meter.

Activities

■ 1. Jerk the magnet quickly in and out of the middle of the cardboard tube several times. Watch the compass. How does the meter react?

_____

_____

▲ 2. Tell two ways in which you could generate more electricity with a magnet.

a. _____

_____

b. _____

_____

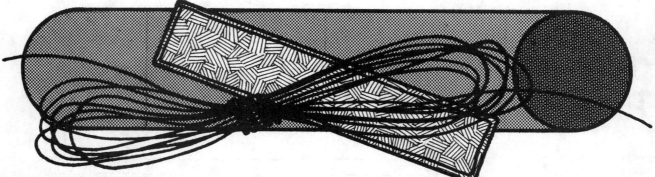

Name _____

POWER CHALLENGE, PART 1

Electricity for your home and school are made by a big system called a **generator**. A generator works in the same way as the magnet and the coil of copper wire. In a generator, water is heated by burning fossil fuels (coal and oil), by nuclear power, or by solar energy. Steam forms. This steam turns a turbine. A **turbine** is a magnetic shaft (**rotor**) inside a coil of copper wire (**stator**). Turning the magnet shaft inside the coil generates electricity.

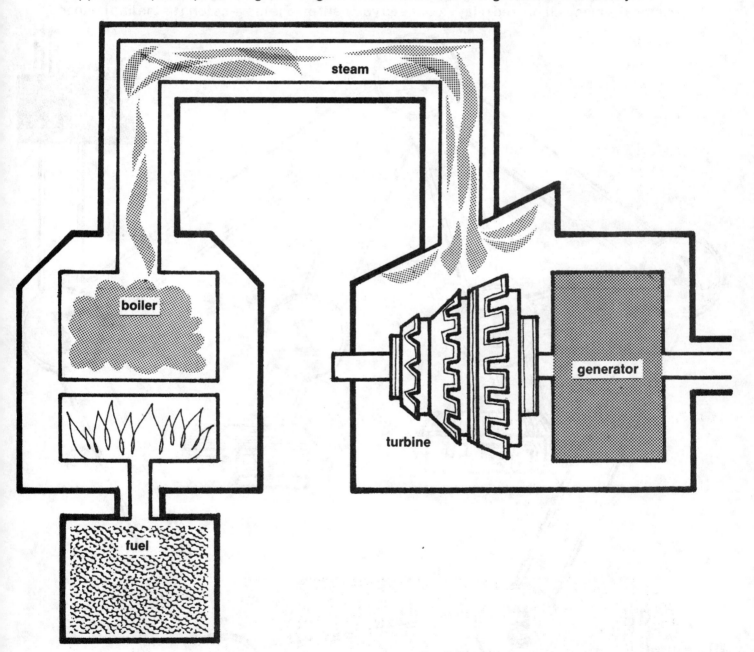

After electricity has been produced by the generator, it travels to relays and passes through a transformer. The **relays** see that the right amount of electricity can flow out to where it is needed. The **transformer** changes the electricity to the correct voltage (strength).

POWER CHALLENGE, PART 2

▲ Activity

Help get the right voltage of electricity to the houses and factories pictured below as quickly as possible. Put a penny (low voltage) on 5 and 7. Put a dime (high voltage) on 1 and 2. Then, try to move the pennies to 1 and 2 and the dimes to 5 and 7 in six moves or fewer without allowing any of the different electric charges to meet. On every move, you can go in any direction. You can cross as many numbered relay stations as you want on one move as long as the line is clear.

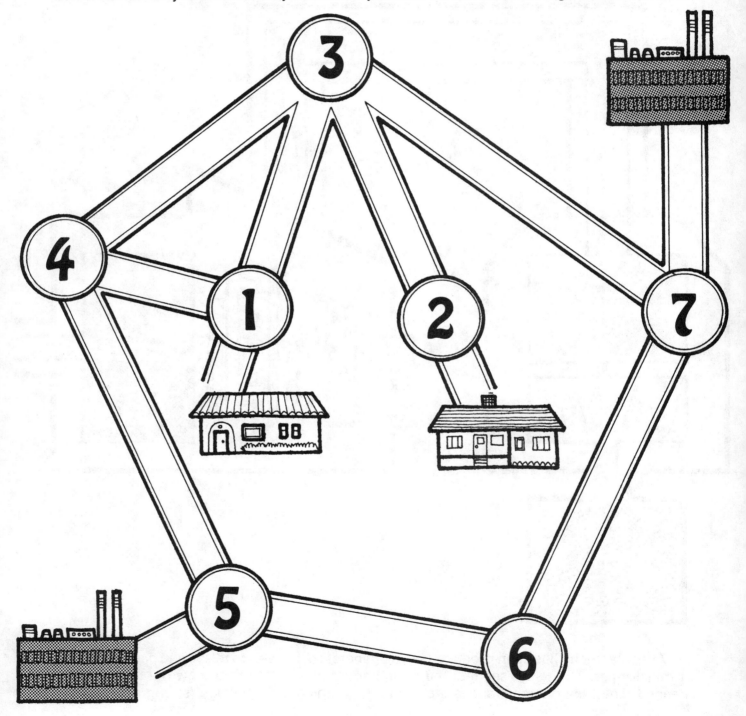

Name _____

OTHER WAYS TO GENERATE AN ELECTRIC CURRENT

There are other ways to generate an electric current. Certain types of material release electrons when they absorb light energy. **Photoelectric** or **solar cells** are made of these types of material.

Some kinds of crystals give off an electric current when they are bent or squeezed. These crystals are used in microphones and record players. Sound waves bend the crystals enough to make them give off an electric current which then travels to the speakers. Chemical reactions can also generate an electric current.

Materials

small glass dish or ashtray
magnesium ribbon
sandpaper
fresh bleach

two brass paper brads
two pieces of insulated copper wire
a flashlight bulb
a clock with a second hand

Instructions

1. Lightly sand the magnesium ribbon and crumple it into the glass dish.

2. Sand the tips of each paper brad.

3. Wrap one end of each wire around the tabs of one brad.

4. Put one brad on either side of the magnesium ribbon in the glass dish.

5. Pour bleach over the magnesium ribbon until it is covered.

6. Check the time on the clock.

Activity

Touch the bare end of one wire to the end of the bulb base. Touch the bare end of the other wire to the side of the bulb base. If the bulb doesn't light, move the wire around on the base.

1. What happens to the magnesium ribbon? _____

_____

2. How long does the bulb stay lighted? _____

_____

3. What has happened to generate an electric current? _____

_____

Name _____

WHAT IS A COMPLETE CIRCUIT?

An electric current always follows the easiest path. In a **circuit**, electrical objects are connected in a loop that allows electricity to flow through them. It is not a **complete circuit** unless the current flows through all parts of the system. It is a **short circuit** if the current can follow a shorter, easier path and skip some part of the system. Only a complete circuit will light a light bulb.

Activity

✳ Look at each of the pictures. Put an **X** in the box next to each system that you think will light the bulb. Then, use the materials listed to test each system. Circle the picture of each complete circuit.

Materials

one D-cell battery
one flashlight bulb
18 cm of thin, insulated copper wire with ends stripped bare

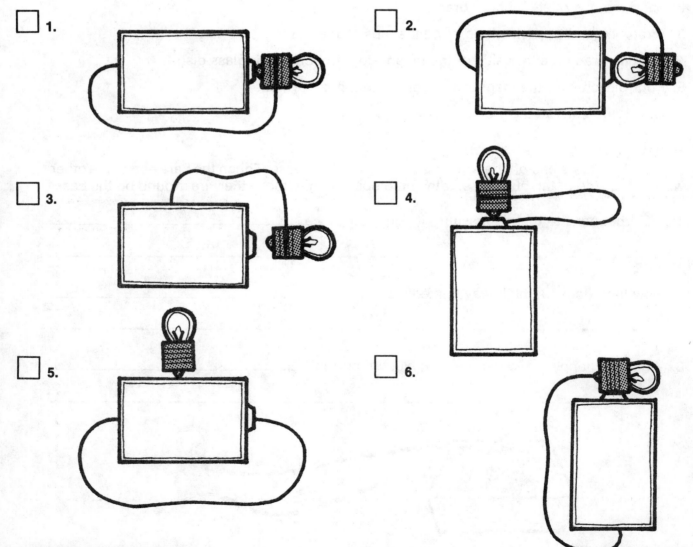

☐ 1.

☐ 2.

☐ 3.

☐ 4.

☐ 5.

☐ 6.

Name _____

CONDUCTORS AND INSULATORS

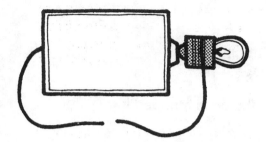

The circuit in the picture is an incomplete circuit. Even a small gap will stop the current flow. What would close the gap and complete the circuit?

High voltage (strong electricity) might jump the gap, but *never* try to attach wires to a wall socket or even a battery more powerful than 12 volts.

Materials that let electricity flow through them easily are called **conductors**. Materials that resist the flow of electricity are called **insulators**. To discover what materials are conductors and what materials are insulators, set up an incomplete circuit like the one in the picture.

Materials

a steel paper clip
a piece of chalk
a plastic ruler
a strip of aluminum foil
a piece of glass

salt water in a glass dish
a piece of cloth
a penny
a piece of rubber
a rock

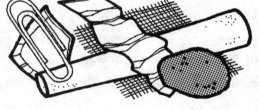

Activities

● 1. Touch the free bare ends of the wires to each of the objects in the materials list to see which ones will complete the circuit and light the bulb. Ask a friend to help you hold the wires or tape them in place with electrician's tape.

■ 2. Fill in the chart to show the results of your tests.

Conductors	Insulators

▲ 3. Make a list of ten other items you could test.

Name _____

CIRCUIT PUZZLE

Materials

two 8½" x 11" pieces of posterboard
a pen
a hole punch
aluminum foil
scissors
two pieces of thin insulated copper wire (about 20 cm long) with the ends stripped bare

clear tape
D-cell battery
one flashlight bulb
electrician's tape

Instructions

1. Space eight holes equally down each side of one piece of posterboard.

2. List things to match in two columns. These can be math problems and answers, antonyms or synonyms, pictures of people in the news and their names, or anything else that interests you. As you list them, mix up the things within each column.

3. Print one column on the posterboard next to each set of holes.

4. Cut the aluminum foil into narrow strips.

5. Place one strip across the back of the posterboard connecting the holes of two matching items. Use clear tape to hold it in place.

6. Repeat this process with the other matches. The aluminum strips may cross over one another.

7. Set up the test circuit like the one in the picture. Use electrician's tape to hold the wires in place.

8. Test each puzzle circuit. A lighted bulb shows a correct match (and a complete circuit).

9. Tape the other piece of posterboard over the back to cover your circuits.

Activities

● 1. Use the circuit puzzle to test your friends.

✶ 2. Make five additional two-column lists of things to match.

■ 3. Based on what you have learned about electricity, explain how the circuit puzzle works.

▲ 4. Use these same principles to design a different electric game or puzzle. Draw a picture or diagram of your game. Then, write step-by-step instructions for building it and rules for playing it.

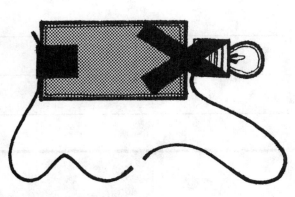

Capital Match	
○ North Dakota	Raleigh ○
○ North Carolina	Atlanta ○
○ Ohio	Nashville ○
○ Texas	Sacramento ○
○ Georgia	Bismarck ○
○ Tennessee	Columbus ○
○ California	Salem ○
○ Oregon	Austin ○

Name _____

SERIES AND PARALLEL CIRCUITS

More than one bulb may be hooked to a single battery. When all of the electricity flows through each bulb in turn, the bulbs are said to be wired **in series**.

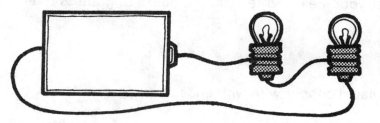

When only some of the electricity goes to each bulb, the bulbs are said to be wired **in parallel**.

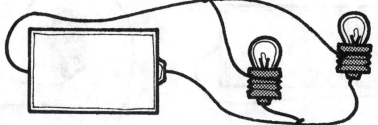

Activities

■ 1. a. Would bulbs wired in a series be equally bright? _____

★   b. Would bulbs wired in parallel be equally bright? _____

    Test each of these types of circuits to see if the bulbs are equally bright. Use electrician's tape to hold the contacts in place. Describe results of your tests.

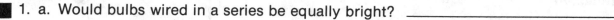

    _____

■ 2. a. In which type of circuit will both lights go out if one light burns out?
★

    _____

    Try it. Use a bulb you know is burned out in place of one of the good bulbs. Retest the series and parallel circuits.

    b. In which circuit do both lights go out? _____

    c. Why? _____

    _____

Name _____

CIRCUIT TESTING

✷ Activity

Predict whether each bulb will be *very bright, bright, dim,* or *out* in these circuits. Then, set up each circuit and test your ideas. Write what the bulb's brightness level is during the test.

Materials

two D-cell batteries
two flashlight bulbs
five pieces of thin, insulated copper wire with ends stripped bare
electrician's tape

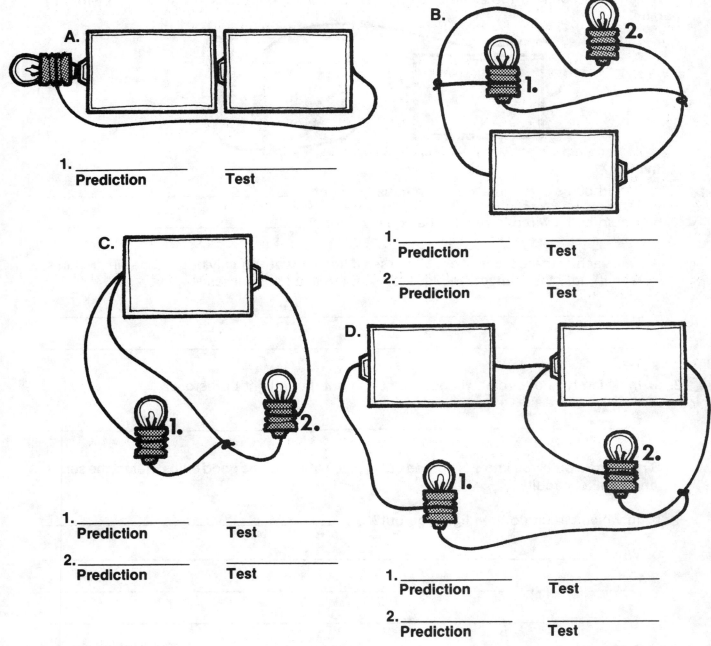

A.

1. _____   _____
   Prediction   **Test**

B.

1. _____   _____
   Prediction   **Test**

2. _____   _____
   Prediction   **Test**

C.

1. _____   _____
   Prediction   **Test**

2. _____   _____
   Prediction   **Test**

D.

1. _____   _____
   Prediction   **Test**

2. _____   _____
   Prediction   **Test**

Name _____

BATTERY POWER, PART 1

Single **electric power cells** are often called batteries, but the term **battery** really means several cells connected together. When batteries are connected **in parallel**, the bottom of one cell is connected to the bottom of the next cell. The top of one cell is connected to the top of the next cell.

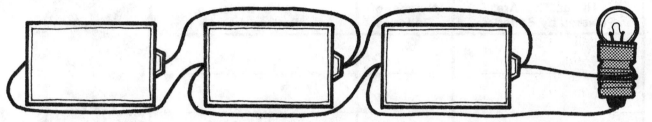

When cells are connected **in series**, the bottom of one cell is connected to the top of the next, because the current in a D-cell battery always flows from the bottom to the top. Wires are not needed for this connection.

Activities

1. a. Which battery circuit system will make the bulb burn more brightly?

_____

b. Test each battery circuit system. Which circuit system actually does make the bulb burn more brightly?

_____

c. Why? _____

_____

2. There is a limit to how many D-cell batteries can be connected together in a series and still increase the brightness of the bulb.

a. What will happen when this limit is reached? _____

_____

b. Why? _____

_____

_____

Name _____

BATTERY POWER, PART 2

■ 3. List six things that are powered by batteries. Tell how many batteries and what voltage (or type of cell) is needed to run each thing. Some things may use more than one type of battery.

Things That Are Powered by Batteries	Number of Batteries	Type of Battery or Battery Voltage

● 4. Play this **High Voltage Game**. Roll two dice for each turn. Add the amounts on the dice and write the total on the first battery. Continue taking turns rolling the dice and recording each score on a battery. You may choose not to use your turn if you do not want the score you've rolled. If you roll doubles, you may use the score on one die or the total of both dice. If you roll double ones, you may take a second turn. The first person to reach a total of fifty (without going over fifty) wins.

Name _____

HOW DOES A SWITCH WORK? PART 1

A **switch** is a way of closing and opening a circuit. A **two-way switch** allows you to turn a light on or off from two different places, such as the top and bottom of a stairway. You can build a two-way switch.

Materials

two blocks of soft wood 15 to 18 cm square
one aluminum pie pan
kitchen scissors
six unpainted short nails
a hammer
two pieces of thin, insulated copper wire 30 cm long
three pieces of thin, insulated copper wire 12 cm long
two D-cell batteries
one flashlight bulb
electrician's tape

Instructions

1. With the scissors, cut two switches and four tabs from the pie pan.

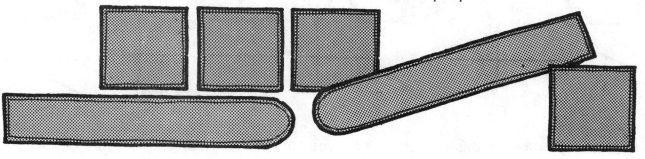

2. Hammer the nails into the tabs and switches to attach them to the wood as shown. Leave enough of the nail above the metal to twist on the wires.

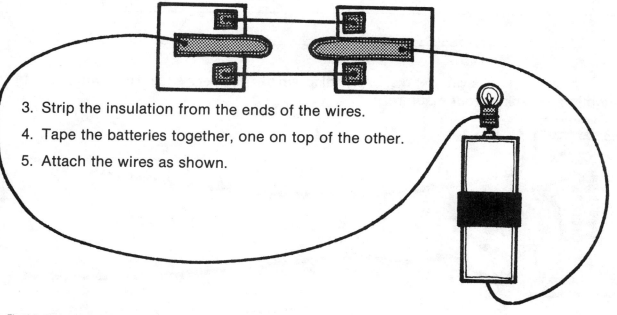

3. Strip the insulation from the ends of the wires.

4. Tape the batteries together, one on top of the other.

5. Attach the wires as shown.

Name _____

HOW DOES A SWITCH WORK? PART 2

✴ Activities

1. Experiment to find out how many different ways you can move the two switches to make the bulb light. Circle each diagram that shows a system which will make the bulb light.

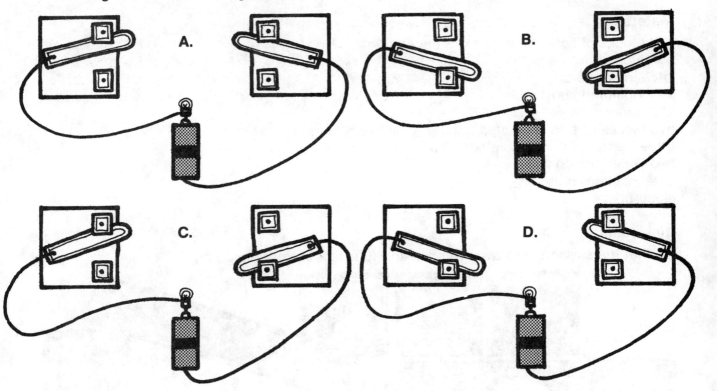

2. List at least three different places where you know that there are two-way switches.

_____

_____

_____

3. Find out how a dimmer switch works. Draw a diagram of a dimmer switch. Then, write a brief description to explain your diagram.

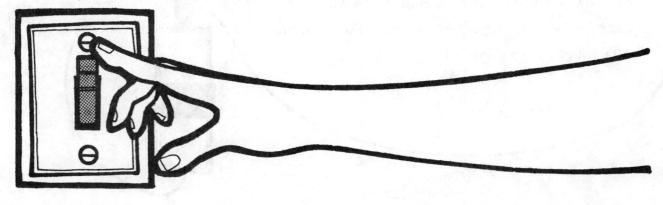

Name _____

YOU CAN MAKE YOUR OWN LIGHT BULB, PART 1

In 1879, Thomas Alva Edison invented the first practical light bulb. Since the early 1800s, scientists all over the world had been trying to produce a light bulb that would burn for longer than a few minutes. Edison was the first to succeed.

Thomas Edison's light bulb is called an incandescent electric lamp because it gives off light when the filament inside gets hot. The hotter it gets, the brighter it glows.

Edison had to solve two problems before he could make his successful version of the light bulb. He had to find the right material for a filament, and he had to keep the filament from burning up too quickly. After testing hundreds of different materials, he found that a carbon filament gave a bright glow. By removing the air inside the bulb (creating a vacuum), he found that he could make the filament last longer.

You can try an investigation similar to the ones Edison performed.

Materials

a pint jar with a large mouth and a lid
a nail
a hammer
electrician's tape
one 12-volt battery
a birthday candle
a small ball of clay
matches
the two-way switch from page 61
a thin strand of steel wool or copper strand wire
two pieces of thin, insulated copper wire 30 cm long with ends stripped bare
a clock with a second hand
ruler

Weather, Electricity, Environmental Investigations
© The Learning Works, Inc.

Name _____

YOU CAN MAKE YOUR OWN LIGHT BULB, PART 2

Instructions

1. Use the hammer and nail to punch two holes in the jar lid about three centimeters apart. The holes should be just big enough for the copper wire to go through.

2. Poke the bare wire ends through the lid far enough to be halfway down into the jar when the lid is on.

3. Form the strand wire or the steel wool into a tight coil.

4. Twist the coil ends onto the ends of the copper wire.

5. Put tape over the lid to hold the wires in place and to seal the holes.

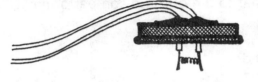

6. Poke the candle into the ball of clay and place it in the jar. The candle should not touch the wires.

7. Attach the wires to the switch and to the battery as shown.

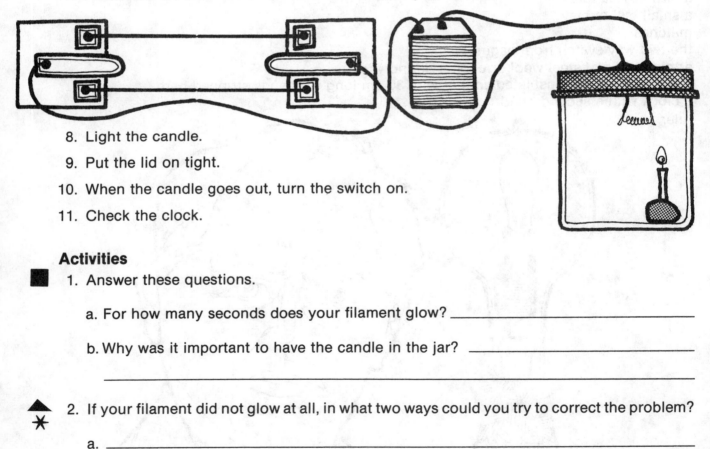

8. Light the candle.

9. Put the lid on tight.

10. When the candle goes out, turn the switch on.

11. Check the clock.

Activities

■ 1. Answer these questions.

a. For how many seconds does your filament glow? _____

b. Why was it important to have the candle in the jar? _____

_____

▲
✶ 2. If your filament did not glow at all, in what two ways could you try to correct the problem?

a. _____

b. _____

Name _____

USING ELECTRICITY TO COPPER PLATE

In this process, called **electroplating**, electricity causes one kind of metal to coat another.

Materials

eight tablespoons of copper sulfate crystals
  (available at hobby stores or drugstores—sometimes called blue vitriol)
two pieces of thin, insulated copper wire 20 cm long with ends stripped bare
wooden spoon   a hammer
a pint jar with a large mouth   a large, clean nail
one 12-volt battery   sandpaper
a copper strip (available at hardware stores)   water

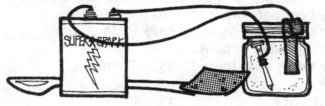

Instructions

1. Pour the crystals into the jar, fill the jar with warm water, and stir until the crystals dissolve. This makes a supersaturated solution. **Supersaturated** means that the water is completely full of copper sulfate.

2. Use the hammer and nail to punch a hole in the copper strip near one end.

3. Twist the bare end of one wire through the hole.

4. Bend the wired end so that the copper strip will hang over the jar edge into the copper sulfate solution.

5. Clean the nail carefully with the sandpaper.

6. Wrap the bare end of the other wire around the nail.

7. Put the nail into the solution.

8. Connect the nail to the negative (middle) terminal of the battery.

9. Connect the copper strip to the positive (outside) terminal.

✱ Activities

1. Explain where the copper that coats the nail comes from. Is it from the water, the copper strip, or both?

   _____

   _____

2. Use encyclopedias or other reference books to learn more about the electroplating process. What other coating metals can be applied in this way? To what base metals are these coating metals usually applied? With what metals or what types of metals is this process most successful? Report your findings to the class.

Name _____

BUILD YOUR OWN TELEGRAPH SET, PART 1

In 1844, Samuel F. B. Morse, an American inventor, made the first telegraph. He discovered that he could send short or long signals by starting and stopping the flow of electricity through a wire. Morse used these long and short signals to make a letter code. Morse code could travel at the speed of electricity (186,000 miles per second). A message could travel over the telegraph lines from New York to San Francisco in less than 1/60 of a second.

You can make your own telegraph set to exchange messages with a friend.

Materials

one 12-volt battery
two pieces of thin, insulated copper wire 33 cm long with ends stripped bare
35 meters of thin, insulated copper wire with ends stripped bare
two pieces of heavy tin or heavy aluminum 15 cm x 2 cm
    (center bottom of a heavy-duty pie pan)
two pieces of heavy tin or heavy aluminum 10 cm x 2 cm
kitchen scissors or tin snips
two pieces of plywood 17.5 cm x 22 cm (1.5 cm thick)
two pieces of wood 4.5 cm square (1.5 cm or a little thicker)
two medium long nails
four long nails
six round-headed screws
a hammer

Name _____

BUILD YOUR OWN TELEGRAPH SET, PART 2

Instructions

Do each step *twice* to make one for you and one for a friend.

The Sounder

1. Use two long, *aluminum* nails to attach one small piece of wood to a larger piece of wood. This forms the base.

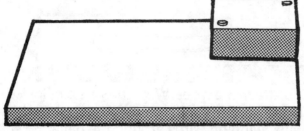

2. Use a nail to punch a hole in the end of one of the longer metal strips.

3. Attach the longer metal strip to the small piece of wood with a screw.

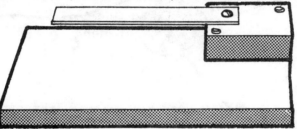

4. Have someone hold up the end of the metal strip while you hammer in one medium-long nail so that it is directly under the end of the metal strip. The space between the metal and the nail head should not be any wider than the thickness of a quarter.

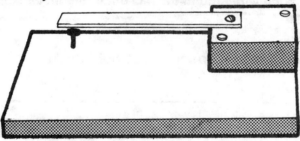

The Key

1. Use a nail to punch a hole in the end of one of the shorter metal strips.

2. Fasten the metal strip to the wood base with a screw.

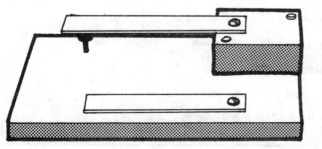

Name _____

BUILD YOUR OWN TELEGRAPH SET, PART 3

3. Bend up the free end of the short metal strip and attach a screw to the wood base directly under the metal strip.

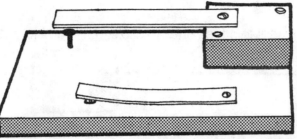

4. Use this diagram to help you attach the wires. Wind the wire clockwise around the nail under the sounder about thirty times, forming a tight coil. Attach the wires as shown under the strips to the screws and nails, winding wires around the nails. Be sure that the winding is from the bottom to the top, ending near the nail head, and that the wire is bare where it makes connections. For longer distances, lengthen the wire and connect additional batteries in series.

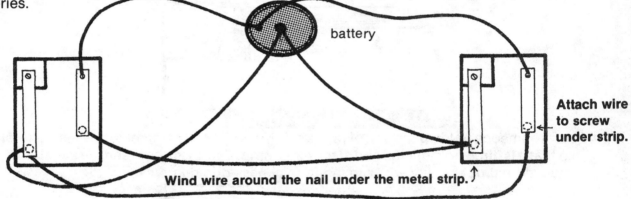

battery

Attach wire to screw under strip.

Wind wire around the nail under the metal strip. ↑

Activity

Use the Morse code to send messages. To send a dot, hold the key down briefly. A dash lasts the length of three dots.

A •—	G ——•	M ——	S •••	Y —•——
B —•••	H ••••	N —•	T —	Z ——••
C —•—•	I ••	O ———	U ••—	
D —••	J •———	P •——•	V •••—	
E •	K —•—	Q ——•—	W •——	
F ••—•	L •—••	R •—•	X —••—	

Comma ——••—— Period •—•—•—

OVER (—•—) is used to mean that you want a reply.

OUT (•—•—•) is used to mean the message is complete.

Name _____

THE MORSE CODE KIDNAPPER

The bank president's son was kidnapped. The kidnappers said that they would send a series of clues in Morse code. If one million dollars was left in locker 22 at the bus station, one more clue would be sent telling how to decode the secret message in the other clues.

The FBI man was very clever. He figured out the secret message before the deadline, rescued the boy, and captured the kidnappers.

Use Morse code to translate the first four clues. Then, see if you can figure out the secret message telling where the boy is being held before you translate the last clue.

1. •—• ——— ••• • •••— • •—• —•——   —•• •— —•——

    _____ _____ _____

    —••• ••— —•—• •— •—• ——— ••• •   —• ——— •——

    _____ _____

2. — ——— •—— •• —• ——— —•• —— •• •—•• •—•• •• ——— —• •

    _____ __

    •—•• •• • • •••— • —• ••• — • •— •—••

    _____ _____

3. ——— —• •—•• —•—• •—•• •— —•—— —•—— —•• ——— ——— • •••

    _____ _____

    ••• —• ——— •—• • ——— •—• ••— ——• •—•• —•——

    _____ _____

    — ——— •• —•—• •••• •••• ——— ——— • •••

    _____

4. •—• •• ••— —• ——— •••— • •—• •— —•• •• — —•—• ••••

    _____ _____ _____

5. ••— ••• • ••—• •• •—• ••• — •—•• • — • •—• ——— ••—•

    _____ _____

    • •— —•—• •••• •—— ——— •—• —•• — ——— —— •— —•— •

    _____ _____

    •—— ——— •—• —•• •••

    _____

MESSAGE: _____

Name _____

THE COST OF USING ELECTRICITY

The electrical energy that your family uses is measured in **watts**. One thousand watts makes a **kilowatt**. Electric companies charge a set price for each **kilowatt-hour** of electricity that is used. The rates vary with the seasons and from company to company.

The electric meter lets you and the electric company know how many kilowatt-hours your family has used. The dials are read from right to left. The first dial shows kilowatt-hours, the next shows tens of kilowatt-hours, the next shows hundreds of kilowatt-hours and so on. Some dials read clockwise, some read counterclockwise. When the needle is between two numbers, it always counts as the smaller number.

Activities

1. Read each of these meters and record the total kilowatt-hours used.

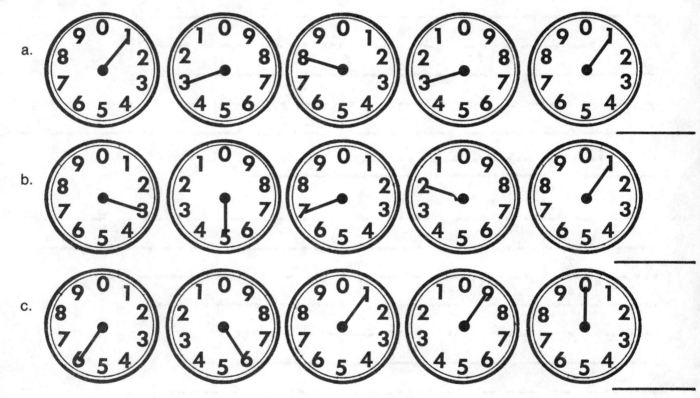

a. _____

b. _____

c. _____

2. If the power company charges .02 cents per kilowatt-hour up to 650 kilowatt-hours and .04 cents for every kilowatt-hour over 650 kilowatt-hours, figure the cost for each of the above meter readings.

a. _____   b. _____   c. _____

Name _____

CAN TAKING A SHOWER HELP SAVE ELECTRICITY?

Materials

a bathtub with a shower
a meter stick
a bar of soap
towel

Instructions

1. One night, take a bath. Run as much water as you like. Before you get in, use the meter stick to measure how many centimeters of water are in the tub. Measure the water level straight up from the drain. (Why is it important to do this *before* you get in?)

2. On the next night, take a shower. Close the tub drain while you shower. When you have finished, get out and measure the water.

3. Record the two measurements.

   a. Bath _____   b. Shower _____

Activities

1. If one centimeter equals one gallon of water, how many gallons did you use?

   a. Bath _____

   b. Shower _____

2. It takes one-fourth kilowatt-hour of electricity to heat a gallon of water. How many kilowatt-hours of electricity did it take to heat the water you used?

   a. Bath _____

   b. Shower _____

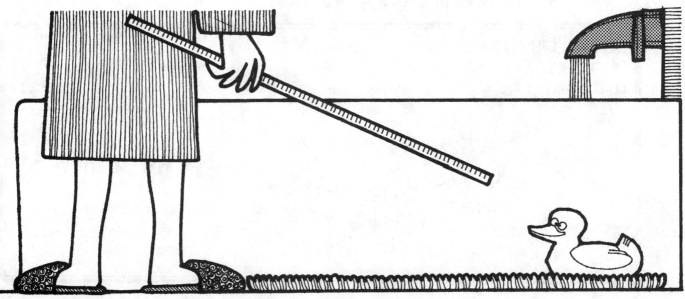

ADDITIONAL INFORMATION SOURCES
AND CORRELATED ACTIVITIES

Additional Sources

Asimov, Isaac. *How Did We Find Out About Electricity?* Matthew Kalmeoff Walker, 1973.

Neal, Charles D. *Safe and Simple Projects with Electricity.* Chicago, Ill.: Children's Press, 1965.

Rosenfeld, Sam. *Magic of Electricity: 100 Experiments with Batteries.* New York: Lothrop, 1963.

Correlated Activities

1. Visit a local power generating station.

2. For a list of experiment booklets that are available free or for a small fee, have students write to:

> Thomas Alva Edison Foundation
> Cambridge Office Plaza, Suite 143
> 18280 West Ten Mile Road
> Southfield, Michigan 48075

3. For a list of books, pamphlets, and experiments about solar energy as a source of electricity, have students write to:

> Solar Energy
> National Solar Heating and Cooling Information Center
> P.O. Box 1607
> Rockville, Maryland 20850

4. Most of the United States' electricity is produced by oil. Find out which countries are the world's leading producers of oil. From which countries does the United States import oil?

5. Coal is also used to produce electricity. Do research to discover which states in the United States produce our coal. On a four-column chart, list the advantages and disadvantages of using oil and the advantages and disadvantages of using coal. Then, compare and evaluate oil and coal as fuels for producing electric power.

6. Do research to discover how nuclear energy is used to produce electricity. On a two-column chart, list the advantages and disadvantages of using nuclear energy.

7. Use the *Reader's Guide* to find articles about what happened at Three Mile Island nuclear generating station. Then, read about several other nuclear generating stations. From your research, list ten to fifteen safety rules that should be followed by the persons operating a nuclear generating station.

8. Choose one of these inventors and write about his life and his experiments with electricity.

   • Stephen Gray (English)

   • Pieter van Musschenbroek (Dutch)

   • Benjamin Franklin (American)

   • Michael Faraday (English)

   • Thomas Alva Edison (American)

9. Interview an electrical engineer about his or her job. Make an appointment and prepare a list of questions you would like to ask. For example, you might want to know what the responsibilities of the job are or what kind of training is required for this career. After the interview, write what you learned in dialogue or narrative form.

10. Interview an electrician about his or her job. Make an appointment and prepare a list of questions you would like to ask. For example, you might want to know what he or she likes and dislikes about the job, what kind of training was required, and what the dangers of working with electricity are. After the interview, write what you learned in dialogue or narrative form.

11. Contact your local power company for the cost of electricity per kilowatt-hour. Then, read your family's meter and keep a record of this reading. Seven days later, read the meter again. Calculate the number of kilowatt-hours of electricity your family used during the week. Then, figure the cost of this electricity.

12. Describe what the world would be like today if the light bulb had never been invented.

13. Pretend there is a blackout and your family is completely without power. Then, describe some of the problems you would have and some of the ways you might solve them.

14. Speculate about the ways in which electricity will be used in the year 2000. Then, describe and illustrate your ideas.

15. Could you survive without any electricity? Write a short paper in which you answer this question and explain the reason for your answer.

16. Analyze and evaluate your family's use of electricity. In what ways is it efficient? In what ways is it inefficient or even wasteful? Recommend some definite changes. With your parents' permission, put these changes into effect. Then, chart or graph the results.

Name _____

POSTTEST

1. Draw a circle around the letter next to each system that would make a complete circuit and light the bulb.

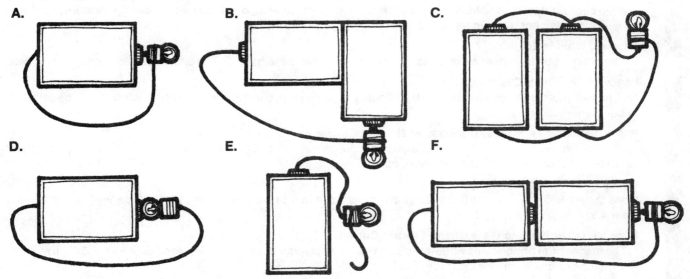

A.   B.   C.

D.   E.   F.

2. Draw in the wires needed to show that the two bulbs are connected in series to the battery.

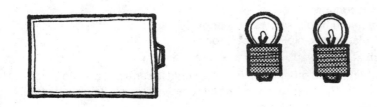

3. From the list, pick the word that best completes each phrase. Write that letter on the line.

A. electrons	D. insulator	G. filament
B. short circuit	E. parallel	H. watts
C. conductor	F. series	I. volts

a. Something that resists electricity flowing through it is an _____ .

b. When all of the electricity flows through each bulb or battery in turn, they are said to be connected in _____ .

c. Electricity is the flow of _____ from one place to another.

d. The use of electricity is measured in _____ .

e. The _____ is the part of a bulb which gets so hot that it glows.

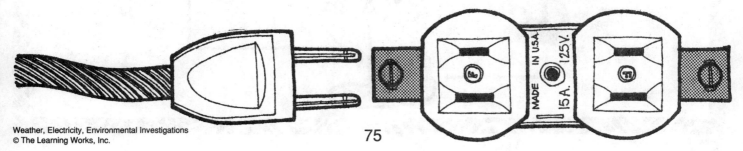

ANSWERS

Page 44, Pretest

1. *Electricity is* electrons flowing from one place to another. 2. *A short circuit happens* when the current follows the easiest path. 3. *An example of a good conductor of electricity is* a steel paper clip. 4. *When some of the electricity goes to each light bulb, the bulbs are said to be connected* in parallel. 5. *A light bulb is called an incandescent light because* the filament inside gets hot enough to glow.

Page 46, What Is Electricity?

1. The charged balloon held close to hair crackles and attracts the hair. 2. The charged balloon clings to the wall.

Pages 47-48, Which Charge Is It?

1a. The two short strips moved apart. 1b. balloon, can, long strip, short strip 2. Test each with a third object known to be uncharged.

Pages 49-50, Can a Magnet Generate an Electric Current?

The compass needle spins. 1. The compass needle moves. (If it does not move, you need a stronger magnet.) 2a. Use a stronger magnet. 2b. Use more coils.

Pages 51-52, Power Challenge

Move dime 1 to 3. Move penny 5 to 4 to 1. Move dime 3 to 4 to 5. Move dime 2 to 3 to 4. Move penny 7 to 3 to 2. Move dime 4 to 3 to 7.

Page 53, Other Ways to Generate an Electric Current

1. The magnesium ribbon turns white and dissolves. 2. Answers will vary. 3. The bleach caused a chemical reaction in which electrons were released from the magnesium.

Page 54, What Is a Complete Circuit?

1 and 6 will light.

Page 55, Conductors and Insulators

Conductors: paper clip, aluminum foil, salt water, penny
Insulators: chalk, plastic ruler, glass, cloth, rubber, rock

Page 57, Series and Parallel Circuits

1a. One bulb will be brighter than the other when they are wired in series. 1b. Both bulbs will be equally bright when they are wired in parallel. 2b. Both bulbs go out when wired in series. 2c. All electricity goes to both bulbs in a series. A dead bulb creates a gap in the circuit.

Page 58, Circuit Testing

A. very bright B. 1. bright 2. bright C. 1. out 2. bright D. 1. very bright 2. bright

Pages 59-60, Battery Power

1. The bulb will burn more brightly when the batteries are connected in series.   When batteries are connected in series, their voltages are added together to determine the total voltage of the system.   The system voltage remains unchanged when the batteries are wired in parallel. 2a. When the limit is reached, the bulb burns out or blows up. 2b. Resistance increases heat until the filament burns up. 3. Answers will vary.

Pages 61-62, How Does a Switch Work?

1. A and B will light the bulb. 2. Answers will vary. 3. There are several kinds of dimmer switches. The simplest is a reostat. The jagged line in the diagram represents the resistor. The loop represents the filament of the bulb. The place the dial is turned to on the resistor determines how easily the power can get through from the power source. The more resistance, the dimmer the light.

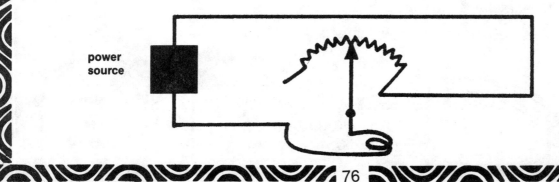

power
source

ANSWERS

Pages 63-64, You Can Make Your Own Light Bulb
1a. Answers will vary. 1b. The candle burns up most of the oxygen to help create a partial vacuum in the jar. With less oxygen, the filament will glow longer. 2a and b. Answers will vary, but the possibilities include making a filament with a tighter coil, making the filament shorter, using two candles to produce a better vacuum, and checking the switch connections to ensure that they are good.

Page 65, Using Electricity to Copper Plate
1. The copper that coats the nail comes from the copper sulfate dissolved in the water. Copper atoms move from the water onto the nail. As this happens, atoms are replaced by copper atoms from the copper strip. 2. Answers will vary.

Page 69, The Morse Code Kidnapper
1. Roses every day buy a rose now 2. To win one million I lie even steal 3. Only lazy dogs snore or ugly tough hogs 4. Run over a ditch 5. Use first letter of each word to make words *Secret message:* Red barn two miles old south road

Page 70, The Cost of Using Electricity
1a. 13831 1b. 35721 1c. 66190 2a. \$.13+\$5.2724 = \$5.402 or \$5.40 2b. \$.13+\$14.0284 = \$14.158 or \$14.16 2c. \$.13+\$26.216 = \$26.346 or \$26.35

Page 71, Can Taking a Shower Help Save Electricity?
Answers will vary, but a normal shower uses less water.

Page 75, Posttest
1. a, c, and f are complete circuits. 2.
3a. D 3b. F 3c. A 3d. H 3e. G

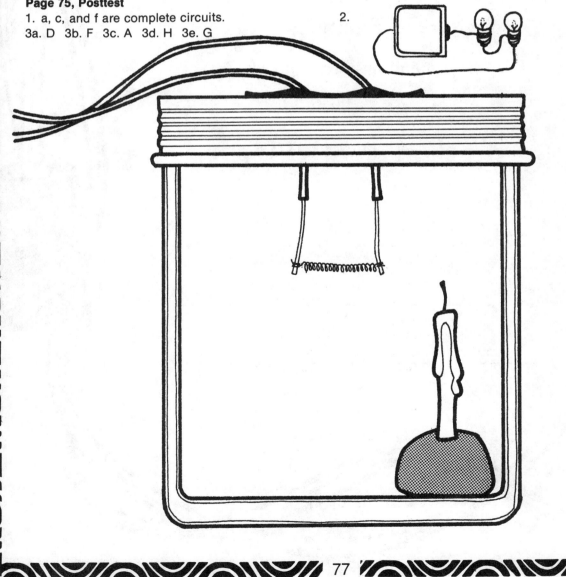

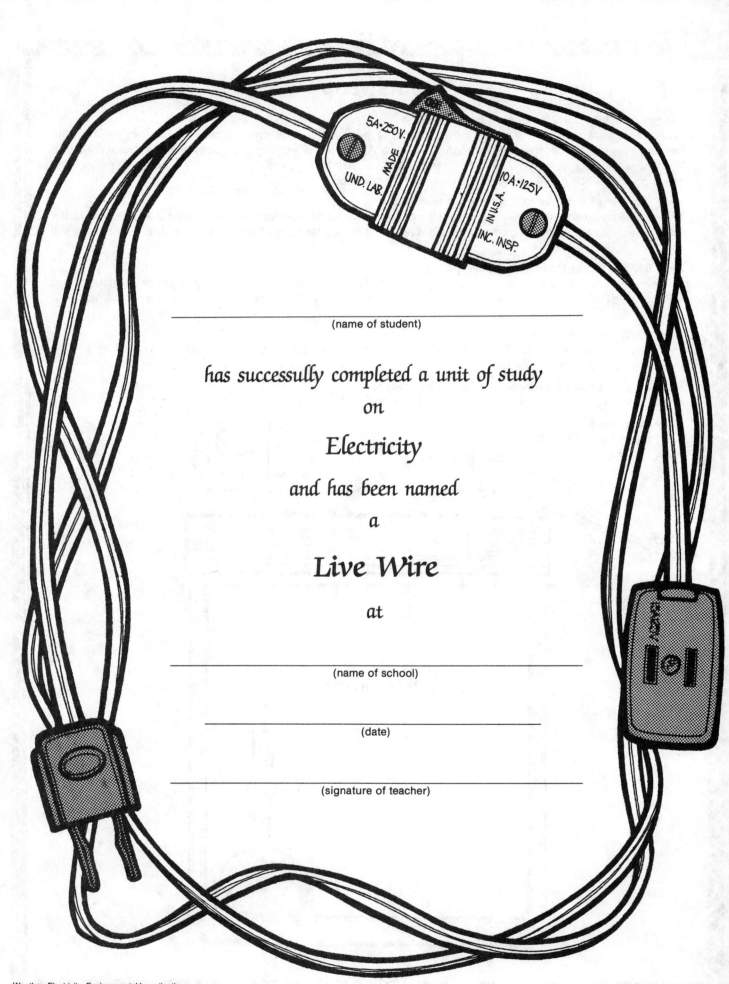

_____
(name of student)

has successfully completed a unit of study

on

Electricity

and has been named

a

Live Wire

at

_____
(name of school)

_____
(date)

_____
(signature of teacher)

BULLETIN BOARD AND LEARNING CENTER IDEAS

1. Label a display area with the question, **Why Do We Like This Kind of Environment?** Put up pictures of particularly nice environments. Include a long sheet of white paper on which students can respond to the question by writing why they like those environments.

2. Encourage students to write about a really enjoyable experience they had outside.

3. Challenge students to find or write poems about a nice environment.

4. Have your students make mobiles that illustrate the main qualities of a nice environment: clean air, pure water, unlittered ground.

5. Display pictures showing how your community used to look. Libraries usually have a collection of old photographs and newspaper pictures that can be copied. Older residents may be willing to help by visiting your class to show pictures and tell about the way the community used to be. Discuss how your community has changed. In your discussion, point out ways that it has been improved, as well as ways that it has been harmed.

6. At an **Environmental Center**, make available activity cards. Instructions on these cards might include the following:

   • What is your favorite spot to go when you want to get away from it all? Describe this spot. Draw and color a picture of it.

   • Find out about at least three animals that have become extinct because man destroyed their environment.

   • If you could go back one hundred years, what *one* thing would you tell people to do differently in handling the environment? Why?

   • Use the *Reader's Guide* to find sources. Then, read to discover what people have done to improve the Great Lakes in the past ten years.

7. Have your students do a neighborhood study and use the questionnaire on page 80 to report their results.

Name _____

NEIGHBORHOOD STUDY QUESTIONNAIRE

Circle the letter of the phrase that best completes each statement about your neighborhood.

1. My neighborhood has

   a. few people.
   b. a medium number of people.
   c. a lot of people.

2. My neighborhood

   a. is open.
   b. is shaded with trees.
   c. has some open areas and some shaded areas.

3. My neighborhood has mostly

   a. big buildings.
   b. homes with yards.

4. My neighborhood is

   a. always quiet.
   b. sometimes noisy but usually quiet.
   c. sometimes quiet but usually noisy.
   d. always noisy.

5. The buildings in my neighborhood are

   a. almost all alike.
   b. almost all different.

Answer each question briefly.

6. The animal I see most often in my neighborhood is a _____

   _____ .

7. When it rains hard, the water _____

   _____ .

8. The thing that I like best about my neighborhood is _____

   _____ .

9. The thing that I would most like to change in my neighborhood is _____

   _____ .

Name _____

PRETEST

Draw a line from the beginning of each sentence to the group of words that best completes it.

1. In a landfill, the microbes break down

2. Things that are biodegradable are

3. Phosphates in detergents pollute

4. Acid rain occurs

5. Plastics are

6. Recycling means

7. Smog forms

8. Litter is

9. An algal bloom is

10. Glass, paper, and metal are

water because they are not easily biodegradable.

when sulfur dioxide and nitrogen dioxide combine with rainwater.

when polluted air stays near the ground.

garbage and return usable nutrients to the soil.

petroleum products.

often recycled.

easily broken down by microbes.

using things over again.

trash that has been carelessly discarded instead of being disposed of properly.

a water-clogging growth of algae.

Name _____

WHAT IS HAPPENING TO OUR ENVIRONMENT?

In 1966, there were waves of soap suds five to six feet high on a stream in Richmond, Virginia. A tidal wave of soap suds rolled down the Susquehanna River in Pennsylvania. In the late sixties and early seventies, a number of beaches along the Great Lakes were closed. The water had become too polluted for swimming.

The disposal of sewage and industrial wastes has become a growing problem. Clouds of polluted air (smog) cling to city skylines. More land is needed each year for houses, shopping centers, and garbage dumps.

Who has been causing all of these things to happen to the environment? PEOPLE.

Activities

1. Find out what the population of your community was two hundred years ago, one hundred years ago, fifty years ago, twenty-five years ago, and ten years ago. Compare these figures with the population of your community today. Use a chart or graph to report your findings.

2. Contact the Department of Public Works or the Sanitation Department to learn how many tons of garbage are disposed of in your community every day or week. Compare this figure with the figures for ten, twenty-five, fifty, and one hundred years ago. How large is the difference? How would you explain or account for the difference?

3. Name the biggest, people-caused environmental problem and suggest three ways in which this problem might be lessened or solved.

_____

_____

_____

_____

_____

_____

Name _____

YOUR SHARE OF THE GARBAGE

Every year, people in the United States throw away 60 billion metal cans, 28 billion glass bottles, 100 million rubber tires, 40 million tons of paper, 4 million tons of plastic, and 3 million junk cars. What is your family's share of the garbage?

Activity ● ■

To find out what your family throws away in one week, number and set out four garbage bags. Ask the members of your family to put metal trash in bag 1, paper items in bag 2, glass and ceramic objects in bag 3, and everything else in bag 4. At the end of the week, weigh each bag. Divide the total weight of each bag by the number of people in your family to get an estimate of each family member's share of the garbage. Then, answer the following questions.

a. How much of each kind of garbage did your family produce in one week?

metal _____

paper _____

glass and ceramics _____

everything else_____

b. What was the total weight of the garbage thrown away by the members of your family in a week?

_____

c. Based on this total, how much garbage would your family produce in a month? _____

In a year?_____

d. How much of each kind of garbage did you produce in one week?

metal _____   glass and ceramics _____

paper _____   everything else _____

e. What was the total weight of the garbage you produced in one week?

_____

f. Based on this total, how much garbage would you produce in a month? _____

In a year?_____

Name _____

TAKE A LITTER LOOK

Litter is any unneeded item that has been carelessly discarded instead of being disposed of properly. It detracts from the beauty of the environment.

Activities

● 1. Go looking for litter. Visit each of the places named on the chart. Without handling the litter, count how many pieces of each kind you see. Then, complete the chart.

LITTER	Where to Look			
	School Yard	Park or Playground	Your Street	Your Yard
Cans				
Bottles				
Junk cars				
Paper				
Plastic items				
Old clothes, furniture, and other things				

✱ 2. Think about the different kinds of litter. Make a table or chart on which you list the ways in ■ which each kind can be dangerous to people's health.

▲ 3. Look through a newspaper or newsmagazine to find an article about the problems caused by ✱ litter or those associated with solid waste disposal. List these problems on a chart and suggest at least one solution for each.

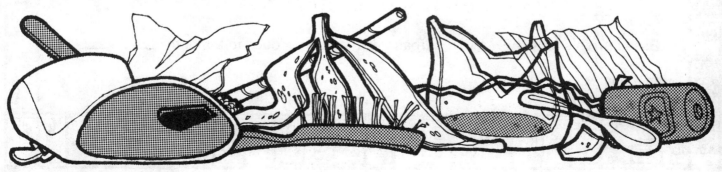

Name _____

LANDFILLS, PART 1

Some communities dispose of solid waste by dumping it in a pit and covering it with dirt. This pit is called a **landfill**. The idea of a landfill is that the microbes (bacteria and molds) in the soil will break down the garbage and return usable nutrients from the garbage to the soil. This investigation will let you see how a landfill works.

Materials

a glass pie plate
a layer of fertile soil
a scrap of bread
a slice of banana

a piece of cooked meat
a piece of paper
a chunk of styrofoam
a piece of plastic

clear plastic wrap

Instructions

1. Spread the soil over the bottom of the pie plate.

2. Lay the pieces of food, paper, styrofoam, and plastic on the soil.

3. Sprinkle with water.

4. Cover with plastic wrap.

5. Punch a few holes in the plastic wrap.

6. Place the covered pie plate in a warm (not hot), shaded place.

7. Check every day for the first fuzzy growth of mold.

Activities

1. To dispose of garbage in a landfill requires a one-acre pit seven feet deep for every ten thousand people each year.

   a. What is the population of your community? _____

   b. How many acres of land would be needed for a landfill for your community for one year?

   _____ For ten years? _____

2. Based on your investigation, answer the following questions.

   a. How many days does it take the mold to grow? _____

   b. Which sample molds first? _____

   Second? _____ Third? _____

Name _____

LANDFILLS, PART 2

▲ c. Seven days after the first signs of mold, describe how the mold has affected each sample.

Bread _____

Banana _____

Meat _____

Paper _____

Styrofoam _____

Plastic _____

3. Things that can be broken down easily by microbes are said to be **biodegradable**. Things that are not biodegradable or that degrade very slowly may remain unchanged for many years. Again, based on your investigation, answer the following questions.

■ a. In general, what kinds of materials are biodegradable?

_____

_____

■ b. In general, what kinds of materials are not biodegradable?

_____

_____

4. When a landfill is covered over, it is often used for building. List and explain some of the problems people whose homes are on a landfill might have.

✳ _____

_____

5. Use the *Reader's Guide* to find sources. Then, read about the hazardous wastes that were buried in an area known as Love Canal. Write about what has happened to the people in the community of Love Canal.

6. Based on what you have observed and read, evaluate the landfill as a safe and sanitary means of solid waste disposal.

◉

Name _____

DO YOU REALLY NEED IT?

There are a lot of things available today that we could live without. When we choose to use them, we waste the natural resources needed to make them. In many instances, we also waste the power required to operate them, and we add to the problem of waste disposal when we throw them away.

Many of these unneeded items are made of plastic or have plastic parts. Plastic is a petroleum product, and disposing of it is a special problem. What happened to the plastic in your landfill investigation? _____

_____

Activities

1. Place several small pieces of plastic in a glass ashtray and put the ashtray into a sink. Cover the plastic pieces with a small wad of paper. Use a match to light the paper. Stand back. **Do not breath the fumes**. Plastic may give off toxic fumes. Let the paper burn out. Then, answer these questions.

   a. How did the fire affect the plastic? _____

   _____

   b. List several reasons we should begin to use less plastic.

   _____

   _____

   _____

2. From old magazines and newspapers, cut pictures of unneeded items that are made of plastic or have plastic parts. Glue these pictures to a piece of cardboard or tagboard to create a poster or montage.

3. Create a montage or poster from the pictures you have cut out, but arrange them from most to least needed or to show which ones require (and, therefore, also waste) power in addition to natural resources.

Name _____

INCINERATION

Some communities burn, or **incinerate**, their garbage. Doing so reduces the volume of the garbage by 80 to 90 percent and the weight by 75 to 80 percent. After incineration, whatever is left is dumped into a landfill. This investigation will help you see how incineration reduces the volume and weight of garbage.

Materials

4 popsicle sticks   a kitchen scale
a wad of paper   a sink
a glass ashtray   matches

Instructions

1. Weigh the ashtray. Record the weight.   _____

2. Break the popsicle sticks into small pieces and put them into the ashtray. Add the paper wad.

3. Weigh the ashtray with the sticks and paper in it. How much do the ashtray, sticks, and paper weigh?   _____

4. Subtract the weight of the ashtray recorded in step 1. How much do the wood and paper weigh?   _____

5. Set the ashtray in the sink.

6. Using a lighted match, ignite the paper and let the fire burn until it goes out completely.

7. After the ashtray has cooled, weigh it again. Record the weight.   _____

8. Subtract the weight of the ashtray recorded in step 1 from the amount recorded in step 7. How much does the ash from the burned wood and paper weigh?   _____

9. What is the difference between the weight of the wood and paper determined in step 4 and the weight of the ash determined in step 8?   _____

10. What percent of the wood and paper weight remains?   _____

11. By what percent was this weight reduced?   _____

Activities

■ 1. Most of the material left after incineration is ash and metal. Explain what slowly happens to metal.

■ 2. In the past few years, the *volume* of garbage has increased far more than the *weight*.
✴ Explain why this has happened.

■ 3. An advantage of incineration is that it reduces the weight and volume of the garbage to be disposed of. Name and explain at least one disadvantage of this disposal method.

Name _____

A SOAPY PROBLEM, PART 1

Detergents are the powdered and liquid soaps we use daily to wash our dishes and clothes. **Phosphates** are added to these detergents to increase the suds and make the suds last longer. But phosphates can cause serious problems. They are not easily biodegradable, and they act as fertilizer to encourage the growth of algae in slow-moving streams and lakes.

Algae appear as a green scum on the surface of the water. A small amount of algal growth is good because fish and other animal life eat the algae. When algae grow too quickly, the result is an **algal bloom**. An algal bloom clogs the water and kills animal life.

This investigation will help you observe how phosphates affect sudsing. You will need samples of three different kinds of detergent. Look at household cleaning aids as well as laundry soaps. Pick samples with different amounts of phosphate.

Materials

3 different samples of detergent (1 tablespoon of each)
3 pint jars with lids
masking tape
centimeter ruler
ball-point or felt-tipped pen
clock with a second hand
water

Name _____

A SOAPY PROBLEM, PART 2

Instructions

1. Pour one detergent sample in each jar.

2. Put masking tape on each jar lid and write the name of the detergent on the tape.

3. Fill each jar half full of water.

4. Screw the jar lid on tightly.

5. Put a strip of masking tape down the side of each jar. With the pen, mark off each strip in centimeters. Then, mark the waterline.

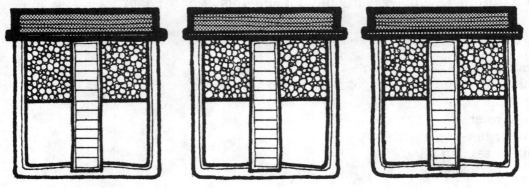

6. One at a time, shake each jar hard for one minute.

7. At the end of the minute, quickly observe the suds level and mark a line on the tape to show how high the suds rose.

8. Record this information on the chart.

Name of Detergent	Percent Phosphate	Suds After One Minute	Suds After Five Minutes	Suds After Ten Minutes

9. Let the jars stand.

10. After five minutes, check to see how much suds is left in each jar and mark a line on the tape to show how far the suds have fallen.

11. After ten minutes, again check to see how much suds is left in each jar and mark a line on the tape to show how far the suds have fallen.

12. Complete the chart.

Name _____

A SOAPY PROBLEM, PART 3

▲ Activities

✱

1. How do the phosphates in household detergents end up in lakes and streams? Draw a chart showing the path water follows from its source in a mountain lake or reservoir into your household and back out as waste water. On your chart, indicate the points at which the water may become polluted and describe the type and effect of this pollution.

2. A small amount of algae is beneficial. A large amount of algae is harmful. Do some research to learn why algal blooms are so destructive to other plant and animal life in lakes and streams. Share your findings with the class.

3. Water follows a natural cycle. It falls on the earth as rain or snow. It soaks into the ground to become part of the water table or evaporates into the air. Water in the air condenses to form clouds and falls to earth again as rain or snow. Read about this natural water cycle. List the steps in this cycle or draw and label a chart to illustrate it.

4. In some communities, waste water is purified and recycled. Find out about this purification process. List the steps in this artificial water cycle or draw and label a chart to illustrate it.

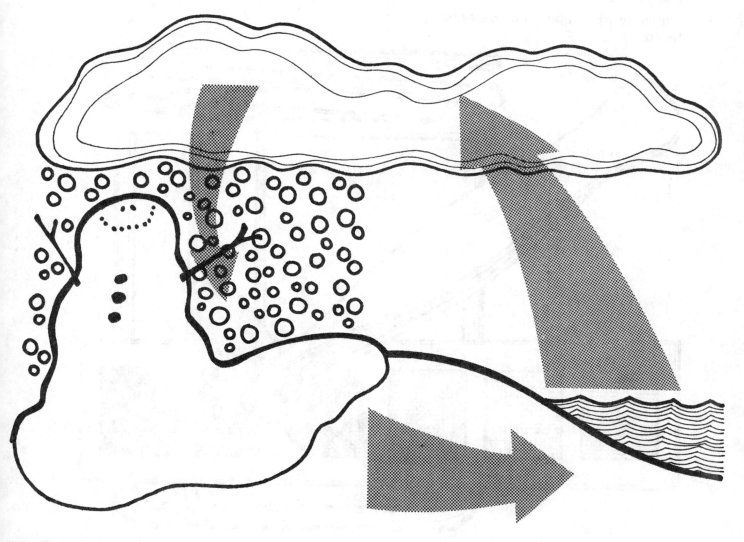

Name _____

BE CAREFUL — IT'S ACID RAIN, PART 1

There may always be plenty of water, but will there always be a supply of *pure* water? Rainwater is an important source of fresh water. Chemicals released into the air from car exhausts and factory chimneys can pollute rainwater before it reaches the ground. These chemicals, sulfur dioxide and nitrogen dioxide, combine with rainwater to form an acid. When this acid soaks into the ground, it dissolves minerals and carries them away. It may also slow plant growth.

Acid rain can run off into streams and lakes. Along with industrial wastes, it is thought to be a factor in preventing fish eggs from hatching and in decreasing the food supply for fish.

The sulfur dioxide and nitrogen dioxide that cause acid rain don't have to be produced where the acid rain falls. They may be produced elsewhere and be carried by wind into low pressure areas.

How can you tell if acid rain is falling on your community?

Materials

widemouthed jar
test tube
litmus, or PH, paper and color chart
tweezers

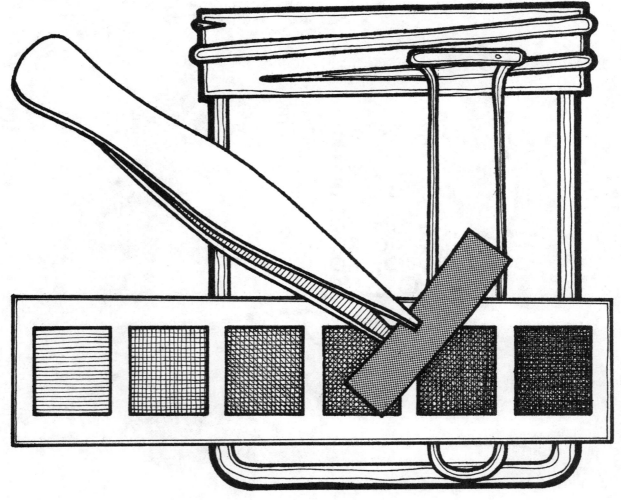

Name _____

BE CAREFUL — IT'S ACID RAIN, PART 2

Instructions

1. Wash and rinse the jar thoroughly.

2. Set the jar outside to collect rain.

3. Immediately after the rain, fill the test tube with collected rainwater.

4. Using tweezers to hold the litmus paper, dip the paper into the collected rainwater.

5. Compare the color of the paper to the chart to find the percent of acidity in the water. Pure water is neutral.

Activities

1. Check three different rainfalls. List the date and results of each test. If possible, also list the wind direction.

Test	Date	Wind Direction	Percent of Acidity
1			
2			
3			

2. In many cities throughout the world, acid rains are damaging buildings and statues. Find out the names and locations of some of these cities and what each one is doing to repair damage done in the past and to prevent similar damage in the future. Share your findings with the class.

3. This maze shows the source of the pollution. Trace the wind path to see which city will have acid rain and how the rain will reach that city.

Name _____

HELP A STREAM, PART 1

To have healthy rivers and lakes, we must have clean streams. Streams are polluted by litter, sewage, wastes from factories, chemicals from farmers' fields, dirt eroded from bare land, and hot water from careless power generating stations.

Adopt a stream in your area. Visit it. Go prepared to wade in and give your stream a careful checkup.

When you arrive, pick a spot where the water is moving slowly. Pound your stake into the shore to mark the site so you can do follow-up checks at the same spot. As you work, fill in the Help a Stream Log on page 96.

Materials

hip boots
a stream screen
a kitchen sieve
tweezers
several pint jars with lids
an eyedropper
masking tape
a ball-point pen
a meter stick
a centimeter ruler
a rope at least twenty-five meters long
   (Tie on strips of cloth to mark meter-lengths.)

a wood stake
a hammer
a thermometer
litmus paper and chart
garbage bags
old gloves or rubber gloves

How to Make a Stream Screen

Materials

two wooden dowels at least one meter long
a piece of fine mesh screen about one and one-half meters long
   and a little less than one meter wide
tacks or a stapler and staples

Instructions

Tack or staple the screen to the dowels.

Name _____

HELP A STREAM, PART 2

Instructions

1. Measure the width of the stream. Tie one end of the rope to the stake and wade across to the other side.

2. Use the meter stick to check the depth near the shore and in midstream.

3. Check the water temperature near the shore and in midstream. Why is it important to check at *both* places?

4. Scoop up one pint of water midstream and mark with masking tape. Allow this sample to settle out. How many centimeters of sediment are on the bottom of the jar?

5. Use the litmus paper and color chart to check whether the water is acid, base, or neutral. Test near the shore and in midstream.

6. Look for signs of algal growth (green scum).

7. Use the stream screen, tweezers, eyedropper, and kitchen sieve to scoop stream life from the water, rocks, and stream bottom. If you find clams, gill-breathing snails, crayfish, and water pennies, the water is fairly clean. Return all living creatures to the stream once you have recorded your finds.

8. While wearing gloves, collect litter along the shore and put it into garbage bags. Count the number of items that are glass, metal, paper, or rubber.

Name _____

HELP A STREAM LOG

Stream Measurements: Width _____

Depth near shore _____

Depth midstream _____

Stream Temperature: Near shore _____   Midstream _____

Particle Pollution: Centimeters of sediment in one pint of water collected midstream

_____

Chemical Pollution: Results of litmus paper test (You may tape dried papers to page.)

Near shore _____   Midstream _____

Algal Growth: Fraction or percent of stream surface covered by algae _____

Types of Animals Found: Draw sketches of some of the animals on a separate piece of paper. If possible, use books to help you identify them and write their names below your pictures.

Litter: How many pieces of each type of litter were collected?

Glass _____   Paper _____

Metal _____   Rubber _____

Other _____   Other _____

What are the main sources of pollution to your stream?

_____

_____

How might you help your stream in its fight against pollution?

_____

_____

Name _____

WHAT'S HAPPENING TO THE AIR? PART 1

What air we have is held close to the earth by gravity. **Air pollutants** are also held close to the earth. Air pollutants may be things we can see, such as wood and stone dust and textile fibers, or the pollutants may be invisible. Invisible pollutants include sulfur dioxide from burning sulfur-rich coal and oil; carbon monoxide from car, truck, and bus exhausts; hydrocarbons from incompletely burned fuels, industries that use petrochemicals, and paint and dry cleaning plants; nitrogen dioxide from boilers and automobile engines; ozone, a poisonous form of oxygen formed when hydrocarbons and nitrogen dioxide react with sunlight; and lead particles from the incomplete combustion of gasoline that contains lead.

Air pollutants can cause headaches, itchy eyes, sore throats, other discomforts and diseases, and even death. Air pollution can blister paint, erode stone, and wear down metal.

Activities

● 1. Think of eight sources of air pollution in your community to add to this list.

gasoline-powered lawn mowers

_____

_____

_____

_____

_____

outboard motors

_____

factories

_____

_____

burning leaves

_____

stone quarry

textile mill

_____

Name _____

WHAT'S HAPPENING TO THE AIR? PART 2

■ 2. Check the visible pollution in your community. Coat the sides of a medium-sized glass jar with petroleum jelly. Place the jar outside high enough off the ground so that kicked up dirt won't affect the test. Leave the jar outside for three days. Then, look at the petroleum jelly and answer these questions.

a. How dirty is the petroleum jelly?

☐ little dirty   ☐ medium dirty   ☐ very dirty

b. Most of the dirt is

☐ wood dust   ☐ textile fibers   ☐ stone dust

■ 3. Make a key like the one shown using a number two pencil. Use this key to grade the smoke coming from at least four different sources of visible pollution. List each source and its grade.

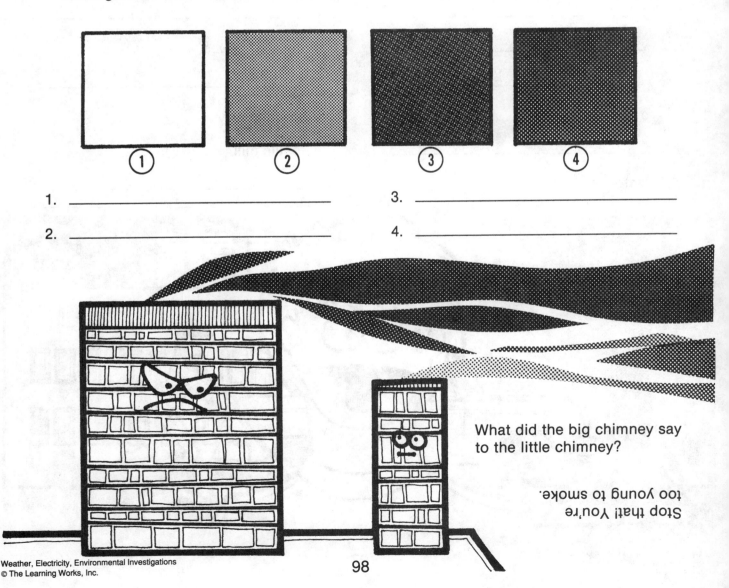

① ② ③ ④

1. _____   3. _____

2. _____   4. _____

What did the big chimney say to the little chimney?

Stop that! You're too young to smoke.

Name _____

RECYCLING

One way to stop adding pollutants to our environment is to use things over again. This is called **recycling**. To recycle trash, materials that can be reused must be separated from those that cannot be reused. This investigation will help you see how this is done.

Materials

a sink
three crackers, crumbled
three glass marbles
one small piece of clear plastic wrap
two tablespoons of iron filings
three nails

an empty three-pound can
matches
a piece of large mesh screen
some newspaper
a magnet

Instructions

1. Put the crackers, marbles, plastic wrap, nails, and iron filings into the can.

2. Mix these things together.

3. Tightly wad up one sheet of newspaper and push it into the can. Place the can in the sink or work outside with water handy to put out the fire.

4. Using a lighted match, ignite the newspaper.

5. Let the fire burn out completely.

6. Let the can cool.

7. Spread out the rest of the newspaper. Lay the screen on the paper and dump what is left in the can onto the screen.

8. Shake the screen gently to sift the ashes.

Activities

Answer the questions below.

● 1. What wasn't burned by the fire? _____

_____

● 2. What didn't pass through the screen? _____

_____

▲ 3. How can you separate the iron filings from the ashes? _____

_____ Try it.

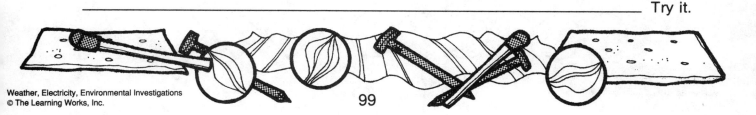

Name _____

FOLLOW THE GLASSPHALT ROAD, PART 1

Blocks made of recycled trash have been used to reinforce the eroded shores of Lake Erie. Metals and glass bottles have been recycled. Glass beads made from trash and mixed in asphalt help roads last longer.

To learn the name of one city that has experimented with glassphalt highways and the state in which it is located, complete this puzzle. Then, unscramble the mystery letters.

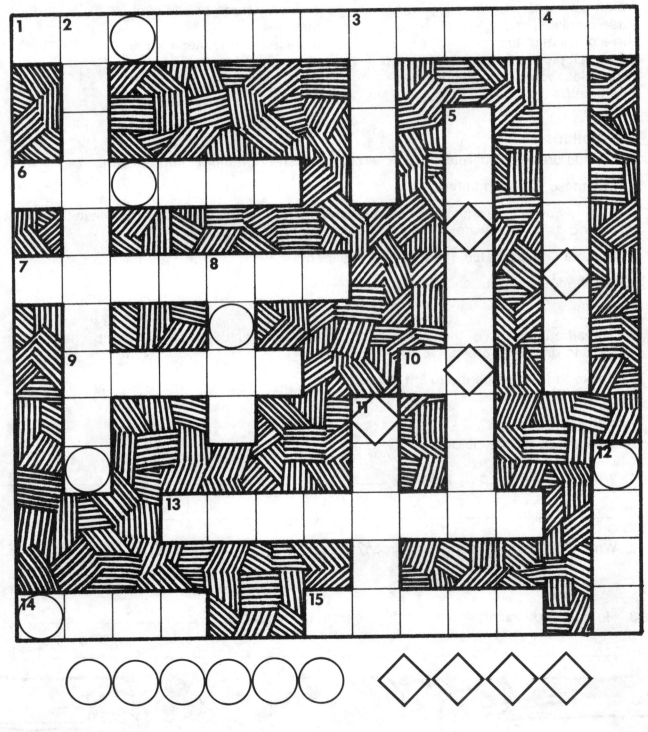

Name _____

FOLLOW THE GLASSPHALT ROAD, PART 2

Across

1. Something that can be easily broken down by microbes is _____ .

6. Trash left where it detracts from the appearance of the environment.

7. To use again.

9. Plant that grows on the surface of streams and lakes.

10. Another name for litmus paper.

13. Molds and bacteria that are found in soils and act as natural recyclers.

14. A type of metal found in certain kinds of gasoline which can pollute the air.

15. Type of trash that can be separated from other trash by burning and, in some instances, by using a magnet.

Down

2. To burn.

3. Substance formed when sulfur dioxide and nitrogen dioxide mix with rainwater.

4. A place where trash and garbage are buried in the ground.

5. Chemical added to detergents to promote sudsing.

8. Type of fuel that may give off sulfur dioxide and pollute the air.

11. A poisonous form of oxygen.

12. Tiny particles of wood or stone that form visible air pollution.

Name _____

RECYCLE YOUR OWN PAPER, PART 1

Materials

a package of cheap paper napkins (not treated for water resistance)
a blender
two teaspoons of liquid starch
a measuring cup
a cake pan
a piece of fine mesh screen smaller than the cake pan
some newspapers
a rolling pin
books
a towel
wax paper
an iron
an ironing board
water

Instructions

1. Tear the napkins into small pieces and put them into the blender.

2. Add two cups of hot water.

3. Blend until smooth.

4. Add the starch and blend again.

5. Pour the mixture into the cake pan.

6. Push the screen down into the pan and move it around until it is covered with pulp.

7. Holding the screen level, lift it out of the pan.

8. Lay the pulp-covered screen on newspapers or on a cooling rack to drain and dry.

9. Peel off the paper sheet and place it on newspapers. If the paper sheet will not peel off, put the screen back into the cake pan, move the screen around, and repeat the process.

10. When the paper sheet is on the newspaper, cover it with newspapers and roll it with a rolling pin.

11. Place books on top of the newspapers and paper sheet. Let the paper sheet sit for about fifteen minutes.

12. Remove the books and the top layer of newspapers. Put a towel over the paper sheet.

13. Place the entire package on the ironing board and iron at a low setting until the paper is dry.

14. Put the paper sheet between two layers of wax paper, place books on top, and let it sit overnight.

Name _____

RECYCLE YOUR OWN PAPER, PART 2

Activities

✳ 1. List some of the ways in which paper is used today.

■ 2. Make a display of as many different examples of paper products as you can find.

■ 3. From encyclopedias and other reference books, find out about the history of paper. In what country was it first made and when? Use this information to write a short book telling the story of paper. Include a table of contents at the front of your book, a bibliography at the back of your book, and a sample of your own recycled paper.

■ 4. Today, many commercial users of paper are conscious of the need to conserve our forests. These firms use recycled paper whenever possible. Look at paper products in a supermarket, stationery or office supply store, or in a greeting card shop to see which ones are made of recycled paper. List and picture some of these products on a chart. If possible, include some actual product samples as part of your display.

■ 5. People have not always known how to make paper. Using encyclopedias or other reference books, find out what substances people wrote on *before* they had paper. Also, find out what writing implements they used. Share your findings with the class.

✳
■ 6. Make a chart on which you compare some of the substances and implements you found out about in Activity 5. What are the advantages and disadvantages of each? Which one lasted the longest? Was the easiest to store? Was the easiest to carry? Was the easiest to use? Was the hardest to use? Was the hardest to erase? Would be most practical today? Would be least practical today? Why?

▲ 7. Make a mosaic using different types and textures of paper.

Name _____

HELP AN ENVIRONMENT

To survive in an environment, animals need food, water, and shelter. More animals can live in an environment that offers a variety of food, plenty of water, and different types of shelter.

Activities

✱ 1. Look closely at your school yard and answer the following questions.

a. What types of food are available? _____

_____

b. Is water available? _____ In what places? _____

_____

c. What types of natural shelter are available? _____

_____

■ 2. Draw a diagram of your school yard showing the natural sources of food, water, and shelter.

✱ 3. List and describe ways in which you could add more natural food, water, and shelter sources. These could include planting trees, planting sunflowers or vegetables, adding a small pond or birdbath, and adding birdhouses and feeders.

▲ 4. List ways in which you would like to improve the environment. Carry out at least one of your ideas.

Name _____

ADDITIONAL INFORMATION SOURCES AND CORRELATED ACTIVITIES

Additional Sources

The following publications are available from Educational Servicing, National Wildlife Federation, 1412 Sixteenth Street, N.W., Washington, D.C., 20036:

Air Pollution
Water, What Would We Do Without It?
Pesticides Are Perilous
Recycling

For a complete list of pamphlets and booklets available from the Environmental Protection Agency, write to:

United States Environmental Protection Agency
Washington, D.C. 20460

Correlated Activities

1. Collect clean trash: paper, plastic bottles, bottle caps, and the like. Don't save anything sharp or rusted. Create a picture, collage, or sculpture from your collected trash. Be as creative as possible. Find pictures of trash art to inspire you.

2. Sponsor an anti-littering poster contest and conduct a clean-up campaign of the school yard or one very needy spot in the community. Take before and after pictures of the site. Contact the Sanitation Department for help in disposing of the collected trash.

3. If the soil in your community is mostly clay, make natural potter's clay and use it to create sculptures.

NATURAL CLAY

MATERIALS: pail   water
clay soil   plastic garbage bag
fine-mesh screen

PROCEDURE:
1. Collect a pailful of clay soil.
2. Strain the soil through a fine-mesh screen.
3. Return the strained clay to the pail.
4. Fill the pail with water, mix well, and strain again.
5. Throw away anything that does not pass through the screen.
6. Repeat this process a second time.
7. Let the dirt settle to the bottom of the pail, and pour off the water.
8. Let the dirt dry until it is just damp. It should be workable without being muddy.
9. Keep the clay covered with a plastic garbage bag until it is needed.

4. Conduct a poll about recycling. Plan to question a specific number of students on each grade level and a specific number of adults. Decide what questions to include. For example, you might ask the following questions:

   a. Do you recycle at home?

   b. Do you recycle at work?

   c. Which reason for recycling is more important to you?
      (1) Saving money
      (2) Reducing pollution
      (3) Reducing the need for additional sanitary landfill sites

5. Find out about community recycling efforts. Organize and sponsor a drive to support one of them.

6. Use the *Reader's Guide* to find sources and then read articles about a recent garbage strike. Find out how the strike affected the community in which it occurred. Report your findings to the class.

7. The United States has 5 percent of the world's population and uses 40 percent of the world's resources. Use encyclopedias and an atlas to find out which countries supply the United States with most of its petroleum, wood, rubber, aluminum, and tin. Consider how this consumption affects the countries that provide the resources. How can the United States begin to lessen its dependency on foreign resources?

8. Plan a community. Make a map of the original plot of land for the community. It should have blocks of trees (taped on so they can be removed later) and a river or lake as a source of fresh water. Include a hill or mountain if you like.

   a. List the major needs of a community. Consider the needs of the environment as well as the needs of the people. Then, decide which parcels of land will be set aside for homes and parks, where shopping centers and schools will be located, and where industries will be allowed to build.

   b. Plan and design separate parts of the community.

   c. Make a drawing or a model (could be to scale) of each part of the community. Add it to the community map.

   d. Decide where streets and highways should be added. Remember, for good drainage, the smaller the area covered by cement, the better.

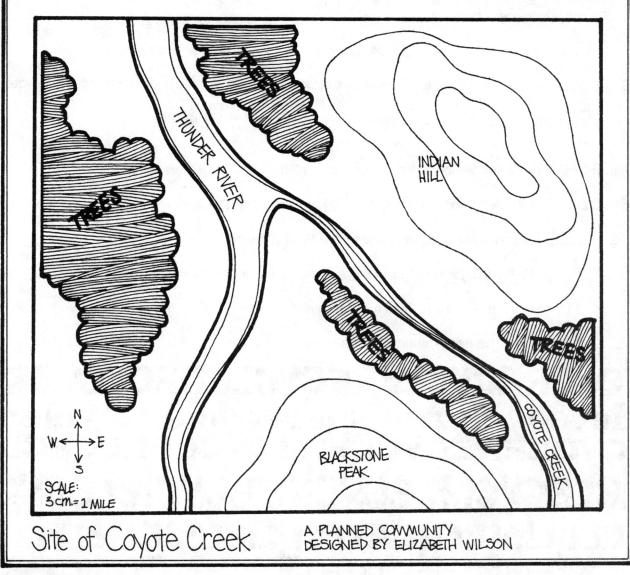

Site of Coyote Creek

A PLANNED COMMUNITY
DESIGNED BY ELIZABETH WILSON

Name _____

POSTTEST

Put an **X** in the box next to the word or phrase that correctly completes each statement.

1. Things that are easily broken down by microbes are _____ .

    ☐ recycled   ☐ biodegradable   ☐ moldy

2. _____ is the chemical in detergents that makes suds hard to dispose of and can cause algal bloom.

    ☐ phosphate   ☐ sulfur dioxide   ☐ ozone

3. Trash that is dumped in a pit and covered with dirt is put in a _____ .

    ☐ lake   ☐ river   ☐ landfill

4. To recycle means to _____ .

    ☐ start over   ☐ use again   ☐ throw away

5. _____ rain forms when sulfur dioxide and nitrogen dioxide mix with rainwater.

    ☐ acid   ☐ basic   ☐ neutral

Number the steps followed in recycling paper to indicate their correct order.

_____ Lift the screen out, holding it level, and let it drain.

_____ Blend water, paper pieces, and liquid starch.

_____ Press the paper sheet between newspapers and iron until dry.

_____ Pour the mixture into a cake pan.

_____ Peel the paper sheet off the screen.

CLERECYCLERECYCLERECYCLER
lerecyclerecyclerecyclerecycler
CYCLERECYCLERECYCLERECYCL
lerecyclerecyclerecyclerecyc
ecyclerecyclerecyclerecyclerecy
ECYCLERECYCLERECYCLERECYCLERECYCLEREC

Name _____

ANSWERS

Page 80, Neighborhood Study Questionnaire
Answers will vary.

Page 81, Pretest
1. In a landfill, the microbes break down garbage and return usable nutrients to the soil.
2. Things that are biodegradable are easily broken down by microbes.
3. Phosphates in detergents pollute water because they are not easily biodegradable.
4. Acid rain occurs when sulfur dioxide and nitrogen dioxide combine with rainwater.
5. Plastics are petroleum products.
6. Recycling means using things over again.
7. Smog forms when polluted air stays near the ground.
8. Litter is trash that has been carelessly discarded instead of being disposed of properly.
9. An algal bloom is a water-clogging growth of algae.
10. Glass, paper, and metal are often recycled.

Page 82, What Is Happening to Our Environment?
Answers will vary.

Page 83, Your Share of the Garbage
Answers will vary.

Page 84, Take a Litter Look
Charts will vary. Litter can be dangerous to people's health because it supplies sources of food and shelter for disease-carrying animals and insects.

Pages 85-86, Landfills
1. Answers will vary. 2a and b. Answers will vary. 2c. The food items will mold and may appear to crumble or dissolve. The paper will become soggy and may start to break up. The styrofoam and plastic will remain untouched.
4. People who build on landfills may have the land sink beneath their houses as the material in the fill decomposes. In addition, toxic wastes, if placed in the landfill, may seep out to poison the air or ground water.

Page 87, Do You Really Need It?
The plastic in the landfill did not change. 1a. Fire melted the plastic. 1b. Answers will vary, but students might point out that we should use less plastic because making plastic uses oil, or petroleum, and because used plastic that is no longer needed is hard to dispose of.

Page 88, Incineration
Answers will vary, but the ash will weigh less than the wood and paper.   The metal will rust.   The *volume* of garbage has increased far more than the *weight* because of the many lightweight but bulky plastic containers being used today.

Pages 89-91, A Soapy Problem
Observations and answers will vary.

Pages 92-93, Be Careful—It's Acid Rain
Test results will vary. Puzzle solution pictured below.

Page 96, Help a Stream Log
Observations and answers will vary.

Pages 97-98, What's Happening to the Air?
Observations and answers will vary, but sources of air pollution might include the following: airplanes, bare dirt fields, bulldozers, burning trash, bushes, cars, restaurants, and many others.

Page 99, Recycling
1. Glass and metal won't burn.
2. Nails and marbles won't pass through the screen.
3. A magnet will separate the iron filings from the ashes.

Pages 100-101, Follow the Glassphalt Road
Across: 1. biodegradable 6. litter 7. recycle 9. algae 10. PH 13. microbes 14. lead 15. metal
Down: 2. incinerate 3. acid 4. landfill 5. phosphate 8. coal 11. ozone 12. dust
The city that has experimented with glassphalt highways is Toledo, Ohio.

Page 104, Help an Environment
Observations and answers will vary.

Page 108, Posttest
1. biodegradable 2. phosphate 3. landfill 4. use again 5. acid
The correct order for the steps followed in recycling paper is:
3. Lift the screen out, holding it level, and let it drain.
1. Blend water, paper pieces, and liquid starch.
5. Press the paper sheet between newspapers and iron until dry.
2. Pour the mixture into a cake pan.
4. Peel the paper sheet off the screen.

RECYCLE RESOURCE

ENVIRONMENT PHOSPHATES

LEAD

INCINERATION

BIODEGRADABLE

This is to certify that

_____

(name of student)

has successfully completed a challenging series of

Environmental Investigations

ALGAE

SMOG

MICROBE

ACID RAIN

LANDFILL

at

_____

(name of school)

_____

(signature of teacher)

_____

(date)

SUDS

LITTER

POLLUTION

DETERGENT DUST

NOTES